How to
Be a Stripper

Secrets to Secure $1000 Shifts

Blake de Louis

Making six-figures from the Midwest to Manhattan

ACKNOWLEDGMENTS

Thanks to my friends Elise and Carmen for their support, encouragement, and motivation, while writing this book. Gratitude to @ButterflyMush, Andrea Acevedo, for the exquisite cover art. Appreciation to the book expert, Melissa Nikohl, for her valuable feedback.

To my beloveds: Nova, Tatiyanna Wynter, and Natasha. Thanks for the sisterhood, and sharing your secrets. Shout out to OG DJ Spicy, Scott Skinner, Larry Scott, and Mike 'Motherfuckin' McClain. Big ups to to Ice Cube for the Player's Club. Striptease and Showgirls deserve a mention.

Thank you to all the assholes in the world who helped push me into this career that has brought me financial freedom; acceptance and love of my sexuality, femininity, and body; the ultimate in flexible scheduling; sexual, physical, and verbal assault; occasional beef with club staff; lots of laughs; and some great friends.

CONTENTS

1 BECOMING A STRIPPER

As a stripper, dancer, entertainer - whatever you want to call it - you will wear many hats. They're probably not the ones most people think. You are, of course, an exotic dancer, so you should be prepared to doll yourself up, dance seductively, and be comfortable in the spotlight.

However, you are also expected to entertain with good conversation, witty banter, and party hosting skills. Further, the high-earning[1] dancers become confidants, psychologists, and a shoulder to cry on for their customers.[2] A well-rounded intellect and personality bode well for this profession. Just ask self-proclaimed stripper hoe,[3] Cardi B.[4]

When working in upscale Manhattan clubs, Cardi often touted her French speaking skills. She was far from fluent, but able to utilize her unique abilities to charm the men into spending more money on her. Acting goes a long way in the stripper world.

The key is to pair social butterfly skills with high pressure sales[5] tactics. This combination is lethal to a man's wallet. Creating an atmosphere of peer

---

[1] The top 1% of dancers at a club, consistently making the most money each shift.

[2] Someone who comes into the strip club as a paying guest.

[3] Song released by Cardi B in 2016 on the 'Stripper Hoe' album.

[4] Former stripper and American rapper, singer, songwriter, actress, and television personality. Born in Manhattan and raised in The Bronx, New York City, she became an internet celebrity after her social media posts and videos backstage at strip clubs went viral.

[5] Selling technique in which relentless and persistent pressure is exerted upon the customer, using psychological pressure to gain a fast sale.

pressure - while you are their only peer, and in a dominant position - guarantees they will say YES and spend.

"Make that Money, Don't Let the Money Make You"
- Ronnie, The Player's Club[6]

Be mentally prepared when you start your stripping career. Strip clubs can be wonderful vehicles for increased self-esteem, financial freedom, and greater work-life balance. Alternatively, they can destroy your body, manipulate your mind, hustle you out of your money, time, and self-respect, and leave you burned out, broke, and bitter.

Get your mind right before you set foot in the club. Eyes on the prize. Always be closing.[7]

Everything Costs

No feelings. No weak minds. Everything costs. Nothing is free.

If you have reservations about convincing someone to spend all of their money, LET THAT CONSCIENCE SHIT GO RIGHT NOW. People love to waste their money on stuff they don't need. If you don't take their money, someone else will - immediately.

If given the chance, customers will always attempt to take advantage of you. Everytime. As a dancer, you are to have no sympathy for customers - ever. If they come in the trap,[8] you take their money. Straight up.

Types of Clubs

There are many types of clubs: topless, full nude, air dance[9] only, full contact,[10] no alcohol, juice bars, BYOB, 18 & up or 21+, early closers and late-night spots, clubs with food, and clubs without. Be informed so you can choose what works best for you. One is not necessarily better than the other - it is all about what you are comfortable with.

---

[6] A revealing, gritty, and funny look at a gentlemen's club, through the eyes of a strong-willed co-ed. Written and directed by Ice Cube in his directorial debut in 1998.

[7] A mantra used in the sales world meaning a seller must always be in the mindset of closing deals, using whatever tactics are necessary.

[8] A place where you make money - the strip club.

[9] Private dances must not include any touching between dancer and customer whatsoever.

[10] Clubs that allow dances and customers to touch each other.

What to Bring

To get hired as a dancer at a strip club, you need to audition. You will meet with the club director[11], where they will assess your physical appearance, talk to you about the club, and have you complete pre-audition paperwork. *You must bring in two forms of ID,* such as driver's license and social security card or passport.

You will be brought to the dressing room to change into your stage costume. Call ahead to ask about costume requirements. Some clubs have rules that stipulate certain heel height, gowns only, or no see-through g-strings. You will be turned away if you don't have the proper attire to audition.

It is unlikely you will be given a locker for your belongings during an audition, so only bring the bare necessities. Do your hair and makeup at home. When ready, notify the director or DJ, and they will add you to the dance rotation and call you up on stage.

Audition

Its normal for everyone to be nervous their first time onstage. Just ignore everyone in the club. Go through your pre-practiced stage routine (see **How to Dance, Ch. 3**). Slowly. Slower.

Dance seductively, as if you were at home alone in your bathroom mirror. Run your hands over your body in slow motion - it can never be slow enough. Feel sexy. When you're more confident, look at the customers and make eye contact as you dance. This is a great way to attract people to your stage.

New Girls on Stage

Customers will approach you, especially if the DJ announces you as an audition. They love new girls. This is one reason its great to stay and work the shift after your audition (presuming you are hired): new girls make bank.

Impressing the Club

The club directors and DJs will be observing you. When you are attracting attention and drawing a spending crowd, they see dollar signs, and are likely

---

[11] Staff running the operations of the strip club, including managing schedules of dancers. Also called the Manager.

to hire you on the spot. You'll then be taken to the office to complete paperwork and choose a stage name. Have a few in mind, in case there is already a dancer using your chosen name.

Accepting an Offer with the Club

Most clubs offer two options: a traditional position as an employee, complete with sick days, and legal healthcare benefits; or a contract as an independent contractor.[12] Read the fine print and ask questions! As an independent contractor, you receive no benefits or wages, and are responsible for your own taxes. However, traditional employment positions at strip clubs are notorious for strict agreements that usually include dancers relinquishing tips and receiving only minimum wage.

Fully read and understand any and everything before you sign it. Request a printed copy to keep for your records.

Scheduling

The flexible schedule is one of the best perks of working as a stripper in the USA. As an independent contractor, you can *technically* work as little or as much as you want. In reality, clubs often blur the lines between independent contractors and employees. They require dancers to perform for minimum shift lengths, or showtimes,[13] - usually six to eight hours - and set and adhere to a weekly schedule.

Independent contractors set their own schedules. You pick your days and time off. There is usually a book in the Directors office where you mark down this information. Some dancers game the system and take off all of the Mondays, or three months everyday in a row. There are many ways to utilize strip club scheduling to your advantage. Just make sure you don't no call, no show.[14]

Don't Be a Strip Club Brat

Go to work enough to stay within the good graces of management. Each club is different, and the rules are different for each dancer - know your club. Some are strict, and you must show up for three shifts per week. Some are ok if you call to let them know you aren't coming. Some don't care what

---

[12] Performs work per a contract with the club. Does not receive wages for services from club, but fees for services directly from customers.

[13] Shifts independent contractor dancers agree to are often called showtimes.

[14] Missing a scheduled shift without calling. Often resulting in contract or employment termination.

you do. Stripping is fairly flexible compared to a square[15] job, so do what you can to keep yourself employed.

Spend Money to Make Money

Strippers pay fees every single shift in order to work, called house rent.[16] This must be paid before the end of your shift, and is sometimes required upon beginning your shift. If you don't earn enough to pay it, your house rent debt accumulates.

Most clubs offer a tiered house fee that corresponds to the number of shifts you agree to work each week. The fee within the tier fluctuates dependent upon day and time. For example:

SAMPLE HOUSE FEE SCHEDULE

Open schedule[17] come & go as you please———		$250 per shift anytime
1 Day/wk ———————————————		$125 per shit anytime
2 Days/wk	$75* Before 7p	$100 wknd/night
3 Days/wk	$40* Before 7p $50 wk night	$75/wknd night
4 Days/wk	$30* Before 7p $40/wk night	$50/wknd night

*$10 if on-site, dressed, and ready to work before club opens in AM.

Indentured Servitude

Certain clubs charge fees in addition to house rent. If you are late to your stage set, they may charge you a fee. If you don't show up for a shift, they may charge your missed house fee, *plus* an additional fee. They can charge fees for whatever is listed in your contract.

Fees rack up quickly, and it can be difficult to dig yourself out of a hole. You become an indentured servant, working everyday just to pay off yesterday's debt to the club. Be aware of your fees! Keep them low, and keep them paid. Don't let the club trap you.

---

[15] Conventional

[16] The amount of money paid to the house by the dancer for each shift they work.

[17] Dancers come to work whenever they please, with no set schedule or required minimum number of days.

TIPPING OUT

Although not outlined in your contract, and often not legal, you are expected to 'tip out'[18] certain staff in the club. It varies from club to club, but the steady three are the DJ, Bartender, and Security escorts from the building at the end of your shift. These are unwritten rules of law you must comply with, in order to work at the club.

The dancers aren't the only hustlers, so don't get smooth talked by a DJ or Bartender who says tipping them 30 percent of your earnings is the norm. We don't work in strip clubs to give it all back in tip outs, and walk home with a pocket full of minimum wage. Be smart.

Determine a set minimal amount to tip each night based upon the service you use. Nobody is helping you on the days your cash flow is negative. Take care of yourself.

Tipping the DJ

Be responsible during your shifts. Check the dance rotation and be aware of your surroundings. Listen for your name, and get to stage on time. Don't make the DJ search the club for you. Learn to adapt your stage routines to any genre of music, and don't request specific songs. Don't ask to be switched around or skipped on the dance list.

Tipping the Bartender

Don't drink. Don't sit at the bar. Don't take up their chairs. Don't ask the bartender for anything. You can still make money for them by approaching men at the bar, and having them buy you drinks. The customers will tip the bartender each time (see **Staying Sober, Ch. 8**).

Tipping Waitresses

Some waitresses will expect a tip from you, or portion of your hourly fee, when running a suite.[19] You should partner with waitresses who understand running a suite is an opportunity *for them* to solicit *their own* tips from customers. You can also work together to extend the suite length (see **Working with the Rest of the Club, Ch. 7**).

---

[18] Money tipped out to strip club staff by dancers.

[19] A private room where dancers spend one-on-one time with a customer. Prepaid by the hour or half-hour. Often comes with champagne, also called champagne or VIP room.

Every time the customer runs their card to pay, they are prompted to press a button, tipping the waitress 20, 30, or even 40 percent. They will press it repeatedly - to the point where waitresses often make more than the dancers themselves. Don't let waitresses hustle you.

It's Not Your Fault the Club Doesn't Pay Staff a Living Wage

Male-run gentlemen's clubs have been around for a long time, and predatory practices abound. For whatever reasons, dancers themselves perpetuate old patriarchal systems, even though they don't benefit from them. Don't let dancers pressure you into parting with your money because "we're a family," or "we watch out for everybody."

Understand that even though club staff may only be paid minimum wage, the club makes more than enough money to increase their hourly rate. The staff deserves a living wage, but not by exploiting the dancer's tips. Do not let them make you feel bad about not tipping them all of your money.

Always remember the strip club is there for you to be able to make as close to a fair wage as you can, being a woman in America. You should be making $1000 nights consistently. Don't ever let this turn into a minimum wage job. Take a break, reassess, and reclaim your power.

Adults Have Choices

If club staff wants to make the money you make, they can do what you do! They don't do what you do, so they don't make the money you make. Dancing is not an easy or safe job, and dancers should not be taken advantage of financially.

Don't tip out all your money. But maintain those relationships by helping the club run smoothly and make money in other ways. Order drinks and encourage customers to tip the staff.

IT CAN HAPPEN TO YOU:

Destinee was broke, working overtime at the mall. She planned to postpone her last semester of college in order to save money for tuition. Instead, her friend brought her to audition at the strip club, knowing it would come natural to her because of her ballerina training. She was right. Destinee made enough money that night to pay for her first tuition installment. She quit the mall the next day and finished school on time, experiencing financial freedom, instead of stress.

In one night, you can go from broke, unemployed, and desperate - to being your own boss, working your first shift, and taking home more cash than most people make in two weeks. Don't be scared.

RATCHET TIP: You can pretend to be new as long as you want. Dancers who have been around for a decade still claim its their first week - if they can tell it will sell the customer on a suite or dance.

BEWARE: Club staff can be vicious when they don't get the tips they want. Grow thick skin and prepare to ignore them talking shit about you. But watch your back.

2 WHAT TO WEAR

More is More

The more to take off, the better. You can make the striptease last longer, and increase your tips. Wear a full bustier, stockings, garter, teddy, g-string, choker, earrings, platform heels, satin panties, and robe ensemble. Remove each piece slowly.

Where to buy? Patricia's. Hustler store. Local sex shop. Walmart. Target. Victoria's Secret. Specialty gown shops. Online stripper boutiques. From other dancers backstage.

Strip Club Fashion Rules

Tacky is good in the stripper world. What will glow brightly under a blacklight? Rhinestones from head to toe sparkle across the stage. Easy on, easy off is a lifestyle.

You can bling out and bring your most over-the-top wardrobe dreams to life as a stripper. Just wear what works for your body, and what *you* feel sexiest in. You will make the most money when you feel confident. And if you're not making money in what you're wearing, just change into another outfit.

Classic Moneymaking Outfits

As cliche as it sounds, the schoolgirl look is a surefire moneymaker. Pleated miniskirt, crop top, white panties, knee-highs, pigtails, and glasses are guaranteed to get loads of cash thrown at you. Bigger spenders are often attracted to a nicer dress with more glamorous make up. Sports-related costumes on game days are popular with crowds.

Having something that sets you apart from other dancers helps get extra attention. It could be as simple as you always wearing bright red lipstick, fuzzy leg warmers, or light up shoes. Or you could take it as far as a belly dancing costume or foreign accent. Make sure its something a customer can remember after a night of drinking.

The Official Stripper Shoe: Pleasers

Pleaser[20] brand platform stripper shoes are simply the best. Tall platform heels are much more comfortable than regular heels, because your foot is at less of an angle. Buy Pleasers - you won't regret it.

You will need tall, thick socks to protect your knees during floor work. Buy these immediately unless you want big bruises. Your local sex supply store should have a good selection. If not, any non-stripper socks should suffice.

G-Strings that Let the Pussy Breathe

Keep a variety of g-strings on hand, with large and small coverage, for different moods on different days. Not too tight, though, because the pussy always needs to breathe.

Makeup

Plenty of strippers wear minimal makeup. And the rest wear a ton. Wear whatever makes you look and feel your best. Whether that's contouring your whole face, or just applying mascara and lipstick - it's up to you. Just don't waste all your moneymaking time sitting backstage in the dressing room doing your makeup. *Come to work to work.*

Multiple Personalities

If you like to change up your look on a whim, keep a selection of inexpensive wigs in your locker. Go from short blonde bob to long, fire-engine red locks in minutes. Hit up the same customers with a new character. Buy inexpensive wigs at neighborhood beauty supplies. Synthetic wigs will last if taken care of correctly.

---

[20] Official stripper brand platform shoes. www.pleasershoes.com

Always Smell Delicious

Perfume is a secret weapon. It is intoxicating to men. Spray it on, get close, and let it do its job.

Nails & Toes Done

Some men will be drawn to you because they want to feel your long fingernails dig into their arms or back, or admire your pretty toes. Make sure your hands and feet are at least presentable, if not manicured and pedicured. Have a customer with a foot fetish? Make sure he gives you an *extra* tip for a special pedicure to "keep your feet looking good for him."

To Shave or Not to Shave?

Freshly shaven legs are heaven, but men are not going to turn you down because you didn't shave this afternoon. Make sure you pamper yourself enough *for you to feel sexy*, but don't pressure yourself to keep up with unreasonable standards. Moisturize and keep it moving. They'll live.

Hairy Situations

The same goes for your bikini line. Thousands of dancers have made thousands of dollars - all while needing a bikini wax. The truth is that *men just don't care*. Again, make sure you feel sexy - so have a pair of lacy boy shorts, or a thicker thong that provides more coverage, on-hand for those days when your bush needs a trim.

Period Power

A woman's menstrual cycle is mistakenly considered a stripper's nemesis. Nonsense. Go to work when you're ovulating - men are biologically attracted to women who are ovulating. You will make more money simply by showing up.

"Period Boobs Pay the Rent" - Jacq the Stripper[21]

Go to work the week before your period when your boobs are swollen. They're bigger, and you'll make more money. To quote the infamous Jacq the Stripper, "Period boobs pay the rent." Warning: they hurt, so don't let anybody touch you.

---

[21] NYC-based stripper, comedian, author, and actress, with her work centering on sex worker experience. www.jacqthestripper.com

Cut it or Tuck it

Go to work on your period - everybody goes to work on their period. Menstrual cups are an option. Otherwise, use tampons. Dancers either cut the string short enough to where it can't ben seen, or tuck the string up into their vagina. It can be difficult to get out sometimes, and a bit messy. But it works.

It's good to have your own tampons, but club dressing rooms normally have a stockpile of (albeit uncomfortable cardboard applicator) tampons on hand, just in case. Don't take it too hard if you bleed on a customer during an unexpected visit from Aunt Flow - it happens to the best of us.

Don't Bring Anything You Don't Want Stolen

Once you've been working at a club long enough, you should be able to get a locker. They are often occupied, but you can sometimes have the club add you to a wait list. Bring in minimal personal items until you have a locker. You'll have to leave your bag out in the dressing room, and your stuff is liable to be stolen.

Rejected auditions are left alone in the dressing room to change back into street clothes, and have stolen items out of spite. Don't bring IDs, debit and credit cards, or excessive cash. You don't need more money than your house rent. Even then, you should be earning that each night, not paying out of pocket.

A Locker, Finally!

Bring a padlock for your locker. If you don't have one, the club may sell them from the office, or in the vending machines. If you forget your combination or lose your key, directors often have the ability to cut the lock off of your locker. Until you have a safe, secure place to store your stripper supplies, you'll have to lug them back and forth. A backpack or rolling suitcase can work well for this.

Stripper Bag & Locker Must-Haves:

- Stage costumes
    - g-strings, lingerie robe, fishnets, thigh-highs, 2-piece outfits, socks
- Pleaser platform stripper heels
- Makeup
- Bag, Garter, or Rubber bands for Money
- Wigs

- Hairbrush, Straightener, Curling Iron, Hairspray
- Hand sanitizer (big jug)
- Slippers or flip flops for dressing room
- Baby wipes
- Makeup remover wipes
- Perfume
- Costume jewelry
- Gum / Mints
- Trap phone and charger
- Headphones
- Healthy snacks
- Extra tampons
- Scissors (to cut tampon strings)
- Water (clubs often don't provide clean drinking water for dancers)
- Towel or blanket to cover dirty chairs backstage
- Jacket / Robe / Blanket (to stay warm when they crank up the AC to force you out of the dressing room)
- Ibuprofen for cramps or headaches
- Money for emergency house rent
- Extra dollars/quarters for vending machine needs
- Naughty suite games to waste time
    - Adult Charades, Table Topics, Cards Against Humanity

Common (Mis)Knowledge

Most people think strippers are dumb sluts who have sex for money, or victims forced to work the pole against their will. This couldn't be further from the truth. Strippers are smart, hardworking, business owners, who use high pressure sales tactics to command large fees in exchange for their time and companionship.

Myths That Shouldn't Keep You From Dancing
(Hint: None of these are true!)

You have to be beautiful.	FALSE!
You have to have smoothly shaved legs.	FALSE!
You have to have a perfect body.	FALSE!
You have to have straight white teeth.	FALSE!
You have to have perky boobs.	FALSE!
You have to have a flat stomach.	FALSE!
You can't have cellulite.	FALSE!
You have to have fake boobs.	FALSE!
You have to have ass shots.	FALSE!
You have to be a good dancer.	FALSE!

You have to know how to pole dance.	FALSE!
You have to know how to twerk.	FALSE!
You have to be skinny.	FALSE!
You have to be thick.	FALSE!
You have to be young.	FALSE!
Your bikini line has to be perfect.	FALSE!
You can't have stretch marks.	FALSE!
You have to have manicured nails and toes.	FALSE!
You have to wear expensive lingerie.	FALSE!
You can't have a regular day job.	FALSE!
You can't strip forever.	FALSE!
Your body can't jiggle.	FALSE!
You have to have sex for money.	FALSE!

The list could go on and on. Every single myth above is completely false. All you need is your personality, smile, and confidence. That's all it takes to be a stripper. Everything else is lighting, drinks, and hustle.

Example #1:

Chanel holds a law degree from a prestigious university and works as a District Attorney. She flies to another state on weekends to work part-time as a stripper, undetected by her day job.

Example #2:

Staci, the self-proclaimed 'resident old bitch,' at a long-standing popular club, is still holding down the day shift in her platform Pleasers well into her 50s - and making good money.

Example #3:

Lots of dancers have fake boobs, but many customers still prefer natural breasts. Liposuction is popular, but a good amount of men will tell you that 'perfect' women intimidate them. They will end up spending lots of cash on more 'real' girls with features such as stretch marks, non-contoured stomachs, and less exotic looks. Everyone has a different type.

IT CAN HAPPEN TO YOU:

Be prepared. Make sure you have your stripper supplies at work, but don't spend a fortune on them, because you never know what you might need to use them for.

Dorothee had a well-known VIP customer offer her $3000 to let him dress up in some lacy lingerie for an hour. She had a locker full of inexpensive stripper supplies, and no problem letting him pay to play in one of her Walmart teddies, an old g-string, some dollar store pantyhose, and a pair of abandoned heels she found in the dressing room. The whole thing cost her less than $20.

As the night went on, he wanted more. Dorothee bought a ratty, used wig for $10 from a dancer backstage, and the customer *loved it*, to the tune of tipping her an additional $2000. Although customers don't usually require personal use of our stripper supplies, this time Dorothee was able to make $5000 - *plus a nice tip* - when she told the customer he could take his entire outfit home (because who wants it back anyway?). She probably would have passed up that money had all her teddies and g-strings been from La Perla.

RATCHET TIP: Some days it seems like the uglier you are, the more money you make. The less you care, the more cash they throw at you. I'm talking about haven't-shaved-in-a-few-days-in-need-of-a-wax-and-wearing-a-shitty-makeup-job-but-in-a-suite-for-five-hours. Men really don't care. Don't stress over impressing them. Just make the sale.

BEWARE: Some people will judge you and treat you differently once they know you're a dancer. Not everyone is your friend. You don't need to tell them everything about your life.

3 HOW TO DANCE

How to Clean a Pole

First things first. Make sure there is a towel and bag of hand sanitizer at the stage. If not, ask the club to provide it. Pump sanitizer onto the towel and clean the pole from top to bottom before touching or climbing. Especially if you are opening the club. Safety first.

How to Dance Like a Stripper

Watch YouTube Stripper videos. There are many to choose from. Learn the basic stripper moves. Then perfect, perform, and repeat.

How to Pop Your Pussy

Squat, with your toes and feet pointed out. Put your hands on your thighs, and poke your butt out. Pop your hips and butt up and down.

How to Jiggly

Learn how to jiggle the fat on your legs and booty without moving your hips. Rotate your thighs inside and out, left to right. Relax your muscles and allow the jiggle.

Practice isolating your glute muscles until you can noticeably flex each one separately, with enough control to visibly pulse them to a beat. Sit on the corner of a mattress with your butt poking out, and practice to your favorite song.

Hold the pole with both hands. Stick your butt out and lean toward the pole, keeping one leg straight while bending the other leg at knee. Standing on the balls of your feet, rotate your bent knee as you shimmy your way down the pole. Shake your booty while you're down there.

Transition to Floor

Transition to floor work. Squat down with legs open, bringing your butt to the floor. Lean back and put your feet in the air. Do a V-spread and jiggle your legs back and forth. Men love this. Come up on your feet into a semi-backbend, and dance your pussy in front of him while looking into his eyes. Graze your fingers over your g-string.

There are a number of positions you can do from here. Remember, you are a nearly naked goddess on stage in front of them basking in flattering lighting. Show yourself off! They love it.

Transition to crybaby[22] and let the customer feel your booty for a second. Lie on the ground and rub on your body. Simulate masturbation and sex. Watch other dancers on stage, and copy their moves. We are all doing the same things, slowly, and fluidly.

Pole Dancing

Unless you're working in a pole-focused club, nobody makes money on the pole. Its a cool skill to have - and a difficult one to acquire, sustain, and perform - but it doesn't make you much money in clubs geared toward suite sales. There are some men who genuinely appreciate the athleticism of pole work, and tip for it, but not many. You can always use the pole as a prop to hold on to and dance around, even if you never climb on it. Pole dancing is in no way a requirement to be a stripper.

How to Work a Crowd on Stage

Assess the crowd while twirling around the pole. Determine the number of people, and how to divide your time in order to reach everyone. Start with customers who have placed the most money on stage.

Dance for each customer and accept their tips. Pout and tell them you'd "rather stay and hang out with them, but have to go dance for everyone else." Look them in their eyes and give them a wink. Move on to the next mark.

---

[22] Facedown on your stomach, one leg long, one leg bent, popping your hip and butt up and down = jiggly.

How to Share a Stage Set

When there are a lot of dancers at the club, the DJ may start doubling up stage sets. This means you may have to share a stage set with a random dancer. The most important thing to do in this situation is to communicate. Always ask them *before* beginning a stage set if they would like to split the tips 50/50, or each collect and keep their own tips. This will prevent arguments later.

Glass on Stage

Occasionally, customers break glassware or beer bottles onstage. Notify club staff immediately. Remove yourself from the area until it is cleaned and wiped down to ensure no shards remain. You do not want pieces of broken glass stuck in your legs. Dancers have had to pay surgeons thousands of dollars to remove them.

IT CAN HAPPEN TO YOU:

Stacy didn't dance in public her entire adult life. Not at a concert, a bar, or a wedding. She was self-conscious and felt out of place. She swore she would never dance in front of anyone, as she was sure people would start staring and laughing.

Until one day, Stacy started dancing semi-naked professionally as a job. Now she'll dance anywhere, anytime, with anyone watching. She knows she looks good, because she gets paid to dance, and she feels confident in her own skin.

You can go from feeling completely unsexy, insecure, and not knowing how to dance at all, to being an ultra confident, seductive, titty-rubbing, lip-licking, booty-jiggling, pussy-popping stage sensation. All it takes is practice. And some YouTube videos.

RATCHET TIP: Practice new moves at home while listening to your favorite songs, and at work when your stage is empty. Watch yourself in the mirror. Know you look great, and that men love it.

BEWARE: Some men will try to steal money off of the stage. Others will grab money from the stage and throw it back on you, to make it seem like they are continuing to tip, so you keep dancing. It is a good idea to move your money out of reach of the customers as soon as they place it on the stage.

4 STRIPPER SALES 101

If you're working a lot, you will see that there is a time and a place for every hustle in this book. When it's busy, dancers can simply walk up to a customer and say, "Let's go play!" They will go, especially during the last two hours or so before close. Guys are fucked up by that time, and there for one thing - to give dancers money! Other times of day require a bit more effort on your behalf. Tailor your sales approach for each customer and situation.

Selling a Fantasy

Once you step onto the floor,[23] you switch on your stripper persona. That means you're happy, dumb, and want to have fun. Its good to prepare a simple backstory to go along with your stage name, but that's about it. Never give out your real name, or information about your actual life.

Your character can range from slutty to classy, depending on the customer. They love a sweet girl who isn't afraid to talk dirty. However, you are not to be controversial, or very smart - never smarter than them. You are selling a fantasy. Always stay in character; sexy tone, flirty body language, and eye contact is vital.

Talk to Everyone

Approach everyone! This one is huge. Your money is going to come from where you least expect it. Make contact with every single customer on the

---

[23] The public area of the strip club where customers, stages, tables, and the bar are located.

19

floor (except club furniture).[24] It's a numbers game - basic statistics. The more times you hear "No," the closer you are to hearing someone tell you, "Yes."

Nathalie used to be shy and have trouble approaching customers. Men would tell her, "I saw you the other night and I really wanted to buy some dances. I kept waiting for you to come to my table, but you never did."

As a dancer, it is your responsibility to approach customers! Never assume someone won't buy a dance. Assume they will. You will never know either way unless you *talk to everyone.*

It Only Takes One

In the strip club world, it only takes one. You don't need to hear "Yes," from a thousand different customers. You only need one.

Layla had a string of customers tell her, "No," during her Tuesday night shift, resulting in her still owing $115 house rent at 4:30AM. She ignored the sting of rejection and kept trying. Then a customer walked in and spent more on her than all the dancers who had been hearing, "Yes," for hours. Stay positive. Nine-hundred people can tell you "No," and the 901st person may give you $4000 with no problem.

All sales are based upon building relationships. Dancers are required to make the customer feel as if they are genuinely enjoying spending time with them, while covertly observing, collecting information, and analyzing their spending habits. It is a delicate balance.

Touch Me, Tease Me

Flash a million dollar smile. Be extremely affectionate with customers. Make eye contact and physical contact as much as possible. Touch their arm, hug them, put your hand on their thigh, sit on their lap, rub your boobs in their face. Introduce yourself.

"Hi, I'm Blake!" Look them in the eye. Ask them their name. Repeat their name. *Remember their name.* Ask, "Is that your *real* name or your *stage* name?" with a smile and wink. This always gets a laugh, and many customers will be less likely to bother you about your real name after that.

Others will still ask "What's your real name?" Resist getting annoyed.

---

[24] Customers who come to the club religiously, sit at the bar, talk to girls, offer to give massages, but do not spend money.

Prepare a 'fake real name' that sounds realistic. Make a big deal out of telling him, with a pinky-promise not to let anyone know, because its a 'secret only you're only sharing with him.'

Say My Name, Say My Name

Say their name as much as possible while looking in their eye and making physical contact. If you forget their name, get them to spell it for you, say you don't believe their age and want to see their ID, or snag a glimpse of their credit card as they pay. Using their name repeatedly in conversation is a secret sales weapon.

Create a Bond

Use the information the customer tells you against them.

If he says his name is Damon, you should say something like: "Ooh, Damon is one of my favorite names. That's the name of the guy who gave me my first orgasm. So sexy."

"I always go for your type" lines also tend to work well. For example:

Race/Culture: "My last boyfriend was Latino. Latino guys are so hot!"

Hobby: "Uh oh, you play guitar? Musicians always break my heart."

Profession: "IT guys always get me in trouble!"

And the tried and true classic: "You look like my ex boyfriend!" Works every time.

The Male Ego

The ego is of utmost importance to a man, and much of their actions are based on it. That's why it's always a good idea to treat them like the king of the jungle - no matter how big of a loser they are. You're there to make them feel good.

Praise is one of the most powerful forms of persuasion. People love to be flattered, even when they know it's fake. You can praise their intelligence, attitude, style, looks, or job. Say things like, "Oh, your job sounds so hard!" Or, "You must be really strong to do that work!"

Pretend they're the smartest, funniest, most interesting man in the world.

Hang onto their every word. Don't question them. Accept their stories and facts, even if you know they are incorrect. Being technical about anything kills the fantasy. Guys want flirting and fun, not a fact checker embarrassing them.

Always Accept a Drink

If he offers to buy you a drink, order one. *But don't drink it* (see **Staying Sober, Ch. 8**). Buying a woman a drink is an important part of a social ritual for most men. It's how they demonstrate they're interested, and your acceptance of the drink indicates the interest is mutual.

Saying you don't want the drink and you'd rather just have the money is exactly the same as saying, "I don't give a shit about you, and I just want your money so I can move on to the next guy." Of course, that's how we really feel, but - remember - dancers are selling a fantasy.

It works best when you accept the drink, spend a song or two chatting over said drink, and then go in for the dance kill. The time you spend (pretending) to drink together together bonds you socially, and makes him more likely to want a dance from you.

Don't Get Fucked Up At Work

When customers buy you drinks, the club makes money, and the waitresses get tips. So keep the drinks flowing, but don't drink the drinks. Dancers who get fucked up at work get fucked - *literally and figuratively* (see **Staying Sober Ch. 8**).

Is He Going to $pend??

If they're ordering a drink and don't offer to buy you one, they're probably tight with their money. You can ask him to buy you a drink. Asking for what you want is a big part of sales. If he says no, that's a big red flag - *sometimes*.

Some men save up their money for a big night with a stripper, but don't budget in extra $15 beers. That's fine, as long as you get the rest of his money. But you need to discern.

Observe everything. Ask what they do for a living. Where did they go to dinner? Find out if they frequent strip clubs. Are they in town for a conference or business trip? What kind of watch are they wearing? Take note of their shoes. How much are they tipping the waitress?

Key to the Promise Land = Wallet Phone or Phone Home Screen

Look in their wallet when they pay for drinks. Do you see cash? If so, you know right away all of that can be yours. An assortment of credit cards? Max them out. Both? You know what to do.

What is on their phone home screen? This provides valuable insight regarding socio-economic status, psyche, and even political ideologies. Adjust your preferences to match theirs, and create conversation that makes it feel like you two are incredibly compatible. This primes him to be more accepting of your sales pitch. For example:

House - Indicates $$. Big or small? Landscaped yard?
Kids - You can *"have kids of a similar age too,"* or *"also be raising a girl."*
Car - eco-friendly Prius, or gas-guzzling SUV? Align your values.
Neighborhood - city or country? High maintenance or down-to-earth?
Pet - Cat or dog person? Either one: *"Me, too!"*
Sports - *"We love the same team! Go Cards/Cubs!"* (whichever they like)
Hobbies - fishing pics or Marvel comics? *"My cousin used to take me bass fishing."* Or, *"Iron Man II is my favorite movie of the trilogy as well!"*

Different Strategies for Different Days and Times

Many factors come into play when determining how to approach each customer. Saturday night after 4am? Don't waste time with pleasantries and small talk. That's a quick, "Wanna dance?" Approaching someone on a Sunday at 6pm requires sitting down, an official introduction, and giving them a little more time than usual.

Sales. Pressure. Scarcity.

Never give away more than three songs time to asses your customers for a dance sale. That's how long an average stage set is - three songs. A little more than nine minutes, but less than fifteen. That's all the time a customer gets get for free. After that, everything costs.

Men will take all the free time you give them, and not give you shit. You have to pressure them. Three songs max. A quick whisper in the ear and a touch on the thigh is worth more than a drawn out, awkward conversation.

If you see a dancer switching off stage and your customer isn't ready to spend yet, you need to go. You have to cut them off after a certain time if they aren't committing with money.

Efficiency. Time is Money.

You will learn the science of assessing a customer's ability and willingness to spend, and attempting to get money out of them - within the three song mark. If they're not ready to spend money by then (and you haven't identified them as a long term prospect for an hour+ suite, which calls for investing a little more time and risk), you should move on.

HOW TO GET THE PRIVATE DANCE[25]

Never ask for the dance. Don't even use the word dance at all. Here's what can happen when you do that:

"Are you ready to do a dance now?" asked in an uncertain tone.

They may reply, "Well, maybe not," because that question lets them say "No."

Only Give Options You Want them to Choose

Instead, tell them what you're going to do, while looking into their eyes and subtly nodding. Speak to them as if they have already agreed. Take their arm and lead them where you want them to go.

Never ask 'Yes or No' questions. Only provide options that you want them to choose. This way, no matter what they pick, you made a sale. If there is another option of saying "No," let them figure that out on their own.

If they say no, learn to not take it personal. They're not saying no to you. They're saying no to your sales strategy. Regroup and try another angle.

How to Sell Dances

Psychologically prep customers to spend a lot. Always refer to *dances* in the plural, and as "spending time" together. Make a statement instead of a question. Try these on your customers:

"Ok, its time to go have some fun now. I'm ready to rub all over you."

"Ok, we are going to go play now. I know you want to."

---

[25] One-on-one dance with customer, paid by the song. Usually performed in a semi-private cubicle in a special area. Sometimes performed on the floor as a table dance.

"It's lame out here, let's go have some real fun."

"I'm ready to dance for you. You're gonna love it, you'll never forget it."

"You seem super cozy, I'd love to be on top of you."

If the club serves food, and they were eating dinner, you can say, "Hey sexy, you look ready for dessert!"

Use the word fun frequently. Tell them they look ready to have some fun. Ask them if they are having fun, and use their response to sell a dance *no matter what they say*.

If they answer, "No," or, "Yes," respond with, "I know you would be having more fun if I was naked in your lap." Tell them they look bored if they are sitting alone at the bar, and say "I can help with that." *Wink*. Be flirty and sexual.

Come Back Later & Use Their Words Against Them

They may say "come back later." Tell them, "Ok, I'll be back to drag you away for naked time!" with a wink and smile. Or, "Ok, when I come back, we're going to have fun!" *Make sure* he says, "Yeah, we will." Then leave! But come back later.

When you return, be dramatic. Hug them like you're old friends. Greet them by name (if you remember). They love this.

Say, "*You said* come back later. Well, it's later, and I'm here! I'm ready! Let's go!" Or, "Alright, since you told me to come back, I did! I follow directions well." Add a wink or coy smile. "Now let's get me naked!" Grab their hand and lead them to the private dance area. This will work.

You can also tease, "I'm here to force you to have a naked girl on top of you, oh the horror!" Smile, grab their hand, and start walking to the private dance area.

Don't Take Maybe For an Answer

Whenever guys say "*Maybe* later," or "*Maybe* next time," it is because of shyness, or not wanting to hurt your feelings with an outright, "No." In this case, you should be able to pressure them into a "Yes." Lean over, put your boobs in their face, and say "I don't take *maybe* for an answer!"

They should laugh and either agree to go for the dance right away, or say, "Ok, yes later!" If they hesitate, start nodding your head and say, "Yes, see its so much easier to say *yes,* huh?!" They will nod their head with you and laugh.

When its time to check in with them, say "Hey it's time for our fun! Remember you *already* said yes!" Giggle. Take them by the hand and lead them to the lap dance area.

How to Secure a Dance from Stage

The customer approached your stage, which means they are interested in you. Secure a tip. Dance for them a bit onstage.

Lean in close and whisper in their ear how much you'd love to go play with them in the back. They should say, "Ok." Tell them you will meet them right after your set is done. Congratulations. You just pre-sold a dance from stage.

EVERYONE Pays Upfront

Cash before dances. From everyone, every time. Trust no one at the club.

As soon as you bring a customer to the private dance area, say, "My dances are $50 each, or sometimes, I do 3 for $100 - but *only* if I like you. So don't tell anyone else." *Wink.* The way you present it makes the customers feel like its a good deal, and they feel special because 'you like them.'

If they complain about paying upfront, coddle them, "It doesn't have anything to do with you personally. We've just had some bad apples, and our club requires everyone to pay first." They should hand over the cash at that point.

Don't worry about losing a dance sale by ruining the mood. Rule #1, *everybody pays upfront.* Otherwise, when it is time to pay after services have already been rendered, you'll be in for a rude awakening.

Customers lie. They will feign ignorance, claim being broke, or that you swindled them. Pre-paying is always the way to go - even when up-selling songs during dances. Just think of the time they're fumbling for that next hundred as a few seconds you didn't have to work.

Selling Multiple Dances

In order to sell multiples, make your customer feel as if they are the center of your world during dances. Use eye contact, soft gasps or whimpers when appropriate, and keep your hands in their hair, on their chest, or wrapped around them. Most guys will go for the second dance, and then that's an easy up-sell to three for $100.

Miss New Booty

Never stop dancing when you are selling an additional song. It is easier for them to agree to keep going if you are still dancing while you ask. Just as another song starts, do something new and sexy that makes it hard for them to want to stop.

Put your boobs in their face or grind sexily in their lap. Remove a new piece of clothing, go all the way to your g-string, or play with your panties, pretending to consider taking them off and showing them your pussy. Even if the customer planned on stopping after one, they won't be able to resist more dances.

What to Say to Turn One Dance into Three... or 15!

Secure another dance as one song is ending by whispering in his ear, "You're so much fun to dance for - let's keep going."

"I bet you can keep going for just one more." After that dance ends, you can say, "See, I knew you could. Let's try just one more..." Repeat.

"I don't want to stop, I'm having so much fun, aren't you?" Nod your head while you look in his eyes, and he should reciprocate with a head nod, and say "Yes."

Try an Up-Sell to a Suite

After the second or third dance, say, ""Oooh, I'm going to have to change my panties later, you're making me wet." This works especially well if you're starting to sweat - or as strippers call it, glisten. That way you can blame the glistening from dancing to 'getting hot for him.'

Keep up the act, telling him, "I feel like we need to go somewhere more private. Let's move to a suite. It's more intimate there, and we can have a better time together." If they agree, grab a waitress and run their card ASAP. Otherwise, you can tell them, "Ok, we can keep having fun here, but next time I'm taking you straight to the back room!" *Wink*.

If they're becoming resistant, try reverse psychology as a last ditch effort. Say, "I'm getting too turned on, I should take a break before I get us in trouble or something. I guess I could do one more, but then I need to cool down. Let's just do one more…Can you handle it?" Breathe a little bit on their neck. They always say yes.

Variety is the Spice of Lap Dances

Don't give away your best dance right away. If you have 10 different positions, only use three for your first dance. Every time the customer buys another dance, mix it up a little and add in a new position by the end of the song. Changing it up can keep them intrigued.

Learn Your Customers!

Gauge which position they respond to best, and close the sale on another song when you're in that position. Usually, it is on their lap, facing away and leaning against them, so you can speak softly into their ear. Or try covering your chest with your hands while you're closing the sale, so they don't get to see your boobs again until they agree.

No, Don't Stop! (Neurolinguistic Programming)

The customer's brain is programmed to think that, "No," means, "No More." Therefore they feel comfortable saying, "No." But when you transform, "No," into, "Don't stop," - "No," means, "Yes!" Customers are still spending money when you get them to say, "No," like this:

"Do you want me to stop?"	"No." =	$$$
"Do you want this to end?"	"No." =	$$$
"Do you need a break?"	"No." =	$$$
"You *don't* want to *stop* now do you?"	"No." =	$$$

When Everybody Wants You

The appearance of being in demand is huge. Customers always want to be with the dancer that is doing nonstop privates. Always be moving. If you are sitting still, it looks like no one wants you, or you're stuck up.

If you're waiting on the floor, chat up another dancer near you. Potential customers see you laughing, smiling, and having fun, which is approachable - as opposed to sitting and staring at them with resting bitch face. The latter makes them feel sized up and insecure.

The Anti-Hustle Brings the Boys to the Yard

Dancers stand out when they provide the opposite of what a customer is already experiencing. To catch the attention of a man who has dismissed multiple dancers, approach him about 30 seconds before you are called onstage. Smile, look in his eyes, and introduce yourself.

Chat innocuously, and be 'surprised' when your name is called to stage, but flit off, unconcerned with him. He will be intrigued by your mysterious appearance, and disappearance, without (seeming to) hustle him. Making yourself unavailable should bring him to tip you on stage.

THEEEE MONEY TIME

Dancers can make money any day and any time. However, to maximize money-making shifts, make sure you work Thursday, Friday, Saturday nights, and stay until close!

The last two hours before the club closes is the money time. The later it is, the more fucked up people are, and the less effort required to sell. If the club closes at 6am, the most (and easiest) money to be made is between 4am - 6am. You'd be surprised how much money someone will take out of an ATM at 5:30am, with just thirty minutes left until the house lights come on.

Go Back to the Well

Go back to the guys you hustled before, and greet them by name. Customers assume strippers only care about the money, so when you come back - with their name - they *always* buy more dances.

If you don't remember their name but remember his face, use pet names, such as boo, baby, sexy, sweetie, honey, or handsome. Even better is to use a nickname that just the two of you know. Greet him as if you remember everything about him. The fact that you remember him at all will aid you in making more money.

Dances or Suites?

You can make money going either way, or utilizing both. Some dancers 'don't have time' for a one-off dance, and only do suites. This is a preference, but not necessarily an economically smart choice. Dances add up all the same, and often have you earning at a higher rate than the suites.

If a dance is $50 for three minutes, that's a pretty good rate. A large suite cut of $400 for an hour is an ok cut. But you may be better off *not* doing small half-hour suites, where you only get a $100 cut. Hustle that down to nine-minutes work by selling three songs for $100, instead of 60-minutes wasted in the small room. It pays to do the math before committing your time.

IT CAN HAPPEN TO YOU:

On Phoebe's first night, a seemingly well-known customer asked her to do dances in the Members Only[26] area. She figured he must be trustworthy, since he frequented the club. Phoebe allowed him to stack dances[27], and keep going, as he assured her he would "pay her when they were finished."

Phoebe's name got called over the speakers and she was summoned to perform a set. She wasn't bought off[28] the floor or in a suite, so she had to get to stage ASAP. They had done eight sets of dances, so her customer's dance tab was up to $800. He promised to go the the ATM and come to her stage.

Phoebe headed to stage and waited for the customer to arrive with the money he owed her, but he never came. He walked out on her without paying. She got scammed out of $800 on her very first shift as a stripper.

That was a tough, yet important, lesson for her to learn. Trust no one at the club, and make everyone pay upfront. Never stack dances. Especially not more than you're willing to do for free - which should be zero!

BEWARE: The Members Only section may seem like a hotbed of big spenders, but unfortunately, the majority of paying Members end up to be cheapskates that want everything for free (and they mean *everything*), all because they pay the club a measly annual fee. Be cognizant of what's going on if you interact with Members. Make them pay upfront just like everyone else, and don't discount!

RATCHET TIP: On busy nights, if a customer is insistent about meeting her outside the club to have sex, Barbie takes their money and runs. She

---

26 Private area of the club where members pay an annual fee for private access.

27 Allowing customers to receive multiple dances without paying for them ahead of time.

28 When a customer pays the club to take a dancer out of the stage set rotation. Dancers usually receive no money from this transaction.

tricks them into believing they can pay the club extra for her to leave early. Or, she gets them to pay her directly the cash she would have made during her shift, leaving her "free to hangout."

She plays the role, takes their address, provides a fake number, and once they give her $1000 cash, she disappears into the locker room to 'change into street clothes' as they leave the club. Barbie then pockets the money and gets back on the floor to work. The customers have no recourse, as they can hardly report themselves soliciting prostitution.

5 CHAMPAGNE SUITES

Suites, champagne rooms, VIP - they all mean the same thing: prepaid, uninterrupted, one-on-one time with your customer. They usually involve personalized service by a waitress (sometimes called a host), a fancy room, and bottles of champagne. The club takes their cut, and the rest goes to the dancer in the form of a dance dollar.[29]

Many dancers are intimidated by the idea of selling suites. They feel like the prices will scare off customers. But the fact is, if you don't offer the suite, they won't know the option exists, and you've already lost the sale.

How to Sell Suites

Believe in your product. Know that you are awesome, amazing, and beautiful, and any guy that gets to spend time with you is lucky. Radiate this throughout your energy.

Tell customers about the suites. Let them know that you would like to spend private time with them. Give them a tour of the suites with a waitress. You can often close the sale during this tour and just stay in the room.

Double-teaming customers with pressure from two dancers makes it easier for you to sell, and harder for the customer to resist. It is also safer to have a friend in the room with you.

Act like the customer is a big spender, and you expect that they will take

---

[29] Certificates available for purchase from club by customers, to be given to dancers. Dancers trade in to club to receive cash, at face value or for a fee.

you into a suite for long periods of time. Talk like you'll be back there all night. Tell them:

"We're going to have so much fun tonight, baby."

"I'm kidnapping you! You're mine for the rest of the night."

"I'm glad I found you. You made my night."

"It's a shame we close at 5:00am!"

You can sell a room that comes with free bubbly by using the line, "Champagne makes me naughty," - while staying completely sober the entire time.

How to Deal with No Sex in the Champagne Room

THE SALE DEPENDS ON EMOTION, NOT LOGIC. Customers spend because they can't resist your sexy. It makes no fiscal sense to do so, but they empty their wallets anyway. If you discuss details before you get your cash or card swipe, you are dead in the water. Keep logic out of the conversation at all costs. Preserve the fantasy.

When a customer asks, "What do I get back there?" he's really saying, "I'm interested and I want to go. Give me a reason - any reason - no matter how lame, but whatever you do, don't let me think logically."

Give cutesy answers. Use innuendos to imply what will happen. Never commit to anything specific. You can say:

"It all depends on the vibe and chemistry. The suites are the most intimate area of the club, with the most privacy. We have our own server who brings us champagne, and guards the room to make sure nobody bothers us. I get taken out of the rotation, so nobody can call me to dance. I'm all yours. We'll have a good time, baby. Let's go have some fun."

Play up the classy card and you will sell more suites. Big spenders usually want the time and attention of a beautiful, classy young woman with a good head on her shoulders - and a naughty side.

Talking About the Price

Start with the most expensive option. If absolutely necessary, you can negotiate down - it is much more difficult to negotiate up. Never act as if the price is excessive, or anything out of the ordinary. Its worth every penny. Normalize the number.

Assume that they're going to buy it. This activates the law of attraction. You believe it. You know it. You just know that this customer has money, he's going to do an hour suite, and give you at least $100 tip for every half hour he spends with you - no problem.

So you're like "Yeah, baby, our suites are $650 an hour. Let's go have some fun."

And they will say, "Ok."

Congratulations! You just closed one of the highest priced sales at your club. But don't get comfortable so quickly. There is more money to be made.

Boss Level Finesse

When the clock starts on the suite, the real finessing begins. The goal is to keep yourself safe and get max money. You should request the customer tip you at the beginning of the suite, and again at the end, starting with a baseline of $100 per half hour, and maxing out at the best you can finesse. (Don't be afraid to go after $500 or $1000 tips. The worst they can say is no. If they say yes, you just came up!)

To ensure you receive a set tip amount, you can 'create your own fee.' If the club charges $650 per hour, you can tell customers your hourly fee is $850. Have them pay the regular room fee to the waitress, and pay you the $200 difference. You can then request a tip on top of your 'created room fee.'

With these rates, you can easily rack up hundreds, or even thousands, of dollars from your customer. But you *do not* have to ratchet up the experience just because you go into a suite. You *do not* have to do anything that goes beyond your boundaries.

Work Smarter, Not Harder

Contrary to popular belief, *There is no sex in the champagne room*. Haters want to believe suites are all about pay-for-play (and sure, that's going to go down in clubs everywhere), but the real hustlers get paid *more* to do *less*. High earning dancers do the same thing in suites that they do on the floor, or in private dances. They just do it in a suite setting, and for a lot more money.

High-Earners in Suites Do:

- Entertain
- Talk
- Listen
- Joke
- Dance
- Cuddle
- Pour Drinks
- Distract

High-Earners in Suites Do Not:

- Have sex
- Kiss
- Take off their panties
- Allow customers to touch their pussies
- Show customers their pussies*

*(unless they are $pending. A quick flash can be negotiated for a hefty fee. Make them pay!)

You Make Your Rules

The club is *your* domain and *you* are the hostess of the suite. *You are in control.* Don't push your boundaries - you don't need to in order to make money. You just need to be a smooth talker.

Pretend like you "really wish that they could [touch you/whatever it is they want to do]," but you don't want to be fired or get in trouble with the law. Blame it on the club if possible.

Don't let the customers get too close for too long, or focus on sex! Change it up. Keep them entertained, and away from you.

Personify dumb blonde and over the top - think Anna Nicole Smith.[30] Now you realize what a great character she played for her chosen career, right? Be intoxicatingly outrageous. Talk, dance, snuggle, then get up for drinks! Toast to a sexy evening. Distract them. Waste time. Repeat.

---

[30] Former American stripper, model, actress, and television personality. Gained popularity in Playboy magazine as Playmate of the Year, and married 89-year old billionaire J. Howard Marshall.

How To Waste Time In Suites

Start with as many clothes on as possible
Toast and cheers to things
Play with the laser lights
Jump on the couches
Adjust the curtains, TV, and lighting
Ask them to show you things on their phone, photos, videos
Bring a naughty game like Adult Charades or Table Topics

Talk + Dance + Snuggle + Pour Drinks + Repeat = Works every time

What to Talk About?

Collect information, find out what motivates them, what is important to them - and ask about that. Lots of lonely men come to the strip club for companionship, and are more than happy to pay for a meaningful conversation in close quarters with a pretty girl. Make them feel heard, listened to, and important.

Go Full Dumb

Get 'excited' to pour and serve the champagne as you refill glasses. Take your time, and make a big show. Accidentally spill it! Fawn over the mess. Emphasize your ditzy persona and drag it out as you buzz around and clean up.

Take your time. Maybe even leave to get a waitress. Tell the customer you have to go backstage to the dressing room to "freshen up" after the spill.

HOW TO STAY SAFE IN SUITES

Take your heels off immediately. Keep them close by so you can grab them by the stiletto and use them as a weapon to protect yourself, if needed. Tell the customer you took them off because your feet hurt.

By being barefoot, you have more control over your balance, and reacting to unexpected movements. But please, protect your feet in the strip club. Make sure you are wearing thigh highs, or some other sexy socks or slippers. Also, some clubs consider dancers without shoes on as soliciting prostitution. Know your club.

Coordinate with the Waitress

Although you likely sold the room by pretending to the customer that the waitress "is your friend," who will "give you privacy," secretly coordinate a plan for how often the waitress checks in on you (see **Working with the Rest of the Club, Ch. 7**). Once you're in the room, make sure the customer knows the waitress has to return to bring the suite certs, drinks, and update you on time. This way you can always have an excuse that "the waitress is coming and you don't want to get caught!"

Right as the suite time is nearing the end, turn up the heat. Get up close and personal, in his favorite position, grinding and whispering in his ear. Work with the waitress to tempt the customer into swiping his card for another hour.

Create Paranoia

Tell the customer you're scared of breaking the rules because:

- the staff randomly checks the dance and suite areas
- the club is outfitted with cameras
- dancers have been getting fired recently for breaking rules
- undercover cops have been posing as customers for prostitution stings
- any other reason you can think of - they won't know if you're telling the truth or not

Say, "If I get fired, I'll have to come live with you and you'll have to pay all my bills!" This should distract them into talking about that possibility for a while, instead of trying to assault you.

Rebuff Assault & Still Get Tips

When they try to take your panties off, pull their dick out, kiss you, touch your pussy, or do anything that crosses your boundaries, and you stop them, it is inevitable that you will hear:

"Oh, I thought that's why we came back here."

Resist the urge to laugh maniacally and say, "Bitch, you *thought!*" while waving around the cash they paid you.

Treat Them Like Toddlers

Instead, use your non-threatening, kindergarten teacher voice and say, "No, we're not going to do *that*, but we *are* going to have fun." Put your boobs in their face, bounce your ass on them, scratch your nails down their arm. A certain portion of men will accept that.

If you coddle them out of their rapey-ness, you can manage to maintain the relationship long enough to get a tip at the end, and keep them from going beyond your boundaries. Its fucking weird. (This doesn't always work because *some men are literal rapists no matter what.*)

If they insist on whining, "but *you said*," - be straight up with them.

"No, I never said that. I said we would have privacy, be close, drink, talk, and dance. I'm beautiful and funny, and we're having a good time right now, baby. This is a great deal." Talk yourself up. Time with you is worth every dollar they spend, plus more.

Expect the Unexpected

The fact is: men who come into the club and go into a suite want to fuck. Expect this; don't get angry, rude, and hostile. Stay in control.

When you tell them no, they're going to be mad and want to fuck with you, sexually assault you, and rape you. Even if you tell them from the get-go, "I'm not doing this, and I'm not doing that," they're still going to try to do lower levels of it, and act innocent and apologize. No. They aren't stupid, they know exactly what they're doing.

These are married men, husbands, fathers who are little league coaches, have their kids pictures on their phones, and tell you stories about their everyday, wholesome lives. When put in the right circumstances, when nobody is looking, just the boy's club, and it's all locker room talk, they will try to take advantage of you. Every time. Be aware, keep your guard up, enforce your boundaries, and get paid.

IT CAN HAPPEN TO YOU:

Tatiyanna did an hour suite with a customer. He was drunk, and kept trying to get her to take her panties off and touch her pussy. She continued to hold him off him throughout the suite, using the techniques in this book. He began to get angry about being rejected, and threatening to leave her for another dancer.

Tatiyanna saw a Hilton Hotel key card in his wallet. She decided to use this information, and his gull, to her advantage. Hiding her annoyance with him, she turned on the stripper charm and said, "Babe, I'm coming to the Hilton later, yeah?

He quickly changed his tune, relaxing back onto the couch, saying, "Yeah baby, you're coming to hang with me, I'm at the Hilton. Let's get you situated and have a drink." They finished their room, and Tatiyanna finessed her tip, purring, "Five-hundred for me 'cause you love me." He said "Of course," and handed over the cash with pleasure.

Tatiyanna's quick thinking and observation skills helped her deescalate the situation from an aggressive customer on the verge of walking out - and turn it into a once-again happy customer, eager to tip Tatiyanna whatever she wanted.

RATCHET TIP: Be careful when going into a suite with a group of customers and dancers you don't know. If the other dancers give away too much for free, or perform extras,[31] your whole strategy can be undermined. Have you and your customer get your own room 'for more privacy,' to keep him from being tainted by the other dancers. You can use your techniques to stay safe, happy, and paid, while the other dancer gets fucked, with no tip, in the other room.

BEWARE: Men can become aggressive when alone. Don't be afraid to end a suite if they get too crazy or you're uncomfortable. 1. Cash out the suite certificate. 2. Tell the Director. Your safety comes first! If you have to walk away from money - do it! *Not all money is good money.*

---

[31] Illegal sexual acts performed by dancers.

6 ASKING FOR A TIP

Ask for tips onstage, at the end of private dances, and before and after suites. Ask for tips for conversations. Ask for tips when customers don't buy a dance. Ask for tips, all the time, for everything. Ask and you shall receive.

How to Ask for Tips Onstage

When customers approach the rail during your set, they will normally place a few ones onstage as an offering. *You can use the toe of your shoe to pull bills back into the middle of the stage, beyond anyone's reach.* Other customers require a little dancing first to coax the tip out of them.

The standard way to ask for tips on stage is to pull out the strap of your g-string, and wait for them to place bills in it. Thank them and smile. Then turn to the other side and do the same thing. If they do not tip you, say, "No tip?" with a pout, and pull your g-string in their direction. This should prompt them to tip you. If not, move on.

How to Ask for Tips During Private Dances

Ask for a tip after they have paid for their dances, but before you begin dancing. Say something sexy and to the point. For example: "Money makes me wet, and the bigger the tip, the better the dance, baby."

Have them continue to tip you with ones (or bigger bills) in your g-string during your private dance, as if you are still onstage. Ask them to make it rain on you in 'their own private dancer show.' Some customers really enjoy this, and you end up with more cash.

At the end of the dance, ask if they had a good time. They will say, "Yes." Respond with, "Wonderful, baby, me, too." Tell them, "Tips are appreciated," or they can "Feel free to tip you if they feel like you deserve it." Since they just said "Yes," they had a good time, they will feel obliged to tip you.

A Closed Mouth Doesn't Get Fed

Don't be afraid to ask for more cash or better tips. A simple "That's all?" with an exaggerated pouty face can get you an additional tip. Or ask for the other bill they are holding in their hand. "Can I have that $20, too? Pretty please?" Leave no stone unturned. Always go for it. The worst they can say is no. If they are out of cash, take them by hand to a nearby ATM.

How to Ask for Tips During Suites

Always solicit a tip at the beginning of the suite. You never know how customers are going to take it when they don't get what they want. Secure a tip while you are on great terms.

Cutesy Lines Work Best

"Let's get the money out of the way so we can really have some fun!"

"I hate talking money, let's get that over with so I can get naked already!"

"Lets get the tip out of the way now baby, so we can have a good time."

"Let's get the tip taken care ahead of time so we don't have to worry about it."

"How much am I supposed to tip?"

When customers ask you what to tip, this is your chance to reach for the stars. Say whatever you can finesse. Feel confident. Know you deserve the biggest, best tips, and that they are going to happily give you that and more. *Expect it.*

If you're not comfortable going for bigger numbers like $500 - $1000 yet, say, "People usually tip *at least* $100 per half hour." Say it like its the most normal thing you've ever heard, like the price of milk. And you have your money.

You can also work in tandem with the waitress. Have them remind the customer to tip you, and you can remind the customer to tip the waitress on any new tabs or purchases (although they have probably already been scammed into a hefty waitress tip at this point - see **Working with the Rest of the Club, Ch. 7**). Waitresses can guilt customers into giving dancers bigger tips by informing them that the club takes most of the room fee.

Gimmie, Gimmie More

Ask for an additional tip at the end of the suite when you're still snuggled up. Get close, look deep into his eyes, whisper in his ear, and breathe on his neck. "Six-hundred for me because I'm your baby?" If they are happy with you, this should be easy to get.

If they were a handsy handful, but you managed to keep them somewhat entertained and pouting at a safe distance, you can reference this to humorously request a tip, since you "clearly have finessing skills."

If they balk at a tip, don't give up. Keep pushing. *Don't accept no for an answer.* Negotiate. List reasons you deserve a tip, pout a little, put your booty and boobs in their face. They will often give in and give you what you want - even if it is just to make you go away.

1-800-GET-CASH

Customers often run out of cash at the club, hit limits on their credit cards, and reach maximums for daily debit card transactions and bank account withdrawals. Another common snafu is a customer's card being flagged for fraud by their bank. This can be triggered by many non-fraudulent reasons, such as multiple charges, or larger than the customer's average charges. Their account will be temporarily frozen, and transactions declined.

Checking the customer's texts and emails should be step number one. There may be a link to click to confirm and allow the purchase. If not, a call to the company is required, using the number on the back of the card.

You'll often encounter a hold time before reaching a representative on the phone, and customers are usually too drunk to focus that long. If you're running their card for a suite, the waitress should be able to facilitate this process while you keep the customer entertained. Remember, each time the customer's card is swiped, the waitresses have an opportunity to finesse an additional tip as well. Work together. You are a team.

Don't Miss Any Dollars

Don't get left out in the cold. Be prepared with electronic payment apps. Almost everyone has a CashApp, PayPal, Google Pay, Venmo, or Bitcoin account. If not, you can help the customer create one on the spot. They can continue to tip you via these apps.

Make sure you have your apps set up under your stripper name, to protect your privacy. Confirm the payment and *immediately* transfer the funds to a bank account or card. Customers are known to attempt to reverse electronic payments the morning after a trip to the club. Protect yourself and cash out the funds as soon as possible.

Money-Making Mantra

Having a high confidence level is the most important factor when soliciting tips. Give yourself a pep talk in the mirror. "Customers love to give me their money. They *always* say yes to me. I'm the highest paid dancer in this club." Create your own Money-Making Mantra and repeat it until it comes true. And then keep going!

When you hit the floor at work, it will show in your walk and energy that you know you're the hottest dancer there. Men will be dying to give you their money. All you have to do is ask.

IT CAN HAPPEN TO YOU:

Paisley was on the floor, flirting with customers, and soliciting dances. The customers she was talking to turned her down. Her ego felt bruised from the rejection, but she smartly set that aside to pivot into a different moneymaking technique.

"Well, I'm sure you'd like to grace my boobies with some cash instead!" she said, smiling. Paisley shimmied her chest expectantly toward them, grazing her nails across her cleavage. They all tipped her, and one even changed his mind on a dance, buying a set of three for $100.

RATCHET TIP: Most men like to feel like they're helping you with something, but not for things like tuition. That won't get you extra cash. Pretend you're saving for a boob job. Or feel out your customer and figure out what will motivate him to tip you.

BEWARE: If you follow the step-by-step instructions in this book, you will become such a profitable dancer that you will never want to quit.

7 WORKING WITH THE REST OF THE CLUB

The staff makes money when you interact with them in the club. You, the dancer, are the prized person here. Each staff member plays a unique supporting role. Learn how to partner with them effectively to make even more cash.

Directors

No two directors are the same. They have individual personalities, working styles, and *favorites*. Yes, stripping is not a regular job, and club directors are not like regular supervisors.

The club has rules until it doesn't. The rules are different for everyone. The rules are subjective, and depend upon the director working. Things are ok - until they aren't. Don't discuss your working arrangements with other dancers. The directors might not give them the same privileges. Expect the unexpected, and roll with the punches.

Flattery, flirting, and right place, right time will go a long way (some dancers even sleep with the staff for preferential treatment!). What works in a professional office does not win you many points in the club, and may even hurt you. However, bringing in a latte for the scheduled director may help you leave your shift early on slow nights.

Always remember - the directors and club do not love you, no matter what. Even *less* than a regular job. Take care of yourself first.

Waitresses

Every time you involve a waitress in a transaction, you are providing them with an opportunity to hustle a tip. If you order a drink through a customer, a waitress usually gets a tip. If you sell your time into a suite, the waitress has the potential to cash in on a large tip with the customer while ringing in the suite. You two work as a team.

The lure of your beauty, sexuality, and sensuality up close and personal in a suite secures the swipe of the card. You two can both pressure the customer to tip a customary 20 percent, 30 percent, or more, for the waitress. Oftentimes the customer doesn't realize they are tipping the waitress and *not* the dancer, so you better hope you vetted your customer correctly and they still have money left over for your dancer tip.

A way around this is to make sure you and the waitress communicate upfront that the suite room fee doesn't include *any* gratuity for the waitress or dancer. Provide options - they can give tips in cash, card, or through the club's version of dance dollars. The waitress handles this transaction, and the customer will be prompted to tip them again. Help them help you help them.

Some waitresses expect a tip from dancers for the time they spend running their suites. This is unnecessary, unless you personally feel it is warranted. Running suites for dancers allows waitresses to finesse extra money during their shifts. If they do or don't, that's ultimately up to them.

'My Friend' Strategy

Make a waitress friend who is sales savvy and understands the partnership potential. They can scout for likely suite sales while serving drinks. Or you can brief the waitress on customer background, and what you sold him, as you walk her over to introduce them. Always communicate what type of pressure is required for each customer.

When selling a customer on a suite, say, "My friend Brittany is waitressing! She's my favorite. She'll run our suite. She's really cool and will give us lots of privacy." They'll fall for it.

If they're down, sell a bit of the waitresses time in the suite to close a sale. "OMG, Brittany has the best boobs. Sometimes she plays with us and let's me get a sneak peek." *Wink*. Waitresses use this added value to ask for increased tips.

Waitresses can be gatekeepers to big spenders. They have their own rolodex of regulars, and perform the emotional labor to maintain the relationships. They can call them to come into the club, and also make or break a sale, if a customer had a good or bad experience with them.

DJs

DJs manage your stage sets. You can request they play you certain songs or genres of music. A DJ can help you maneuver around an impending stage set when you'd rather earn money in a private dance. DJs can do many things for you. But remember, each service costs. The more you use the DJ, the bigger cut of your cash they will expect.

Some DJs will demand 10 percent and beyond for their services. Some dancers are constantly making requests of the DJs and tip them hundred of dollars. Some dancers do not ask them to do anything beyond what the club requires, so they do not tip extravagantly.

Even if the DJ only makes $5 from each dancer, that's still an extra $50-$100 per shift. Sometimes that's more than the dancers make.

Bartenders

The more space you take up at their bar, and the more drinks you request (unaccompanied by a customer), the more tip the bartender will want. Bring your own bottled water backstage and don't sit at the bar without a customer. Don't ask the bartender for anything. Tip minimally.

Security Escorts

Tip the going club rate. Usually $5 for a standard escort to vehicle. More of a tip is required if they are valeting, heating, de-icing your car, or picking up food and lattes during shifts. Thank them!

KNOW YOUR RIGHTS

Club staff are not your boss. You are an independent contractor (unless you're an employee). Don't let anyone tell you what to do, unless you know for sure they are supposed to. This information will be detailed in your contract.

Miscellaneous club staff do not have any reason to be hanging out in the dressing room. Changing toilet paper, soap, paper towels, unclogging a toilet, or carrying a dancer's bags - fine. But just chilling or hitting on dancers? No.

Your house rent pays the club to provide you with a private dressing room for changing. Ask loitering staff to take their conversations elsewhere. Feel free to close the dressing room door.

You don't have to let club staff touch or hug you. They should be treating you like regular co-workers at a job. Not in a sexual manner. Sexual harassment from co-workers or supervisors at a club is still valid sexual harassment.

Private Dance Staff[32]

Do not tip the private dance staff. If you have to pay the club a cut of your private dances, you may want to watch them cash out the number of dances on the computer before you walk away. They can record a smaller number of dances than you actually performed, and pocket the rest of the cash. You don't want the club coming after you for any private dance discrepancies due to them 'stealing tips.'

Hair and Makeup Artists

Don't use them. Tip minimally, if required. Do your own hair and makeup. Men don't care. Make sure *you* feel confident. Save your money (see **Money, Ch. 10**).

House Mom[33]

Tip minimally, if required. If you have to tip them, you better use them. And if you use them, you better tip them!

Other Dancers

Working with other dancers is inevitable, even if you don't plan on it, don't want to, and don't know any of them. A customer may walk in and choose three dancers who have never met, and ask them to do a suite. Of course you'll say yes.

Dealing with other dancer's boundaries can be difficult, but remember, you already have the suite money. You should have also secured a tip upfront.

---

[32] Club staff who supervise the private dance area and receive club dance fees from strippers.

[33] Usually a former dancer, residing in the dressing room, with supplies, info, and potentially, advanced customer hookups.

Don't push your boundaries, even if the other dancers are doing more.

Partner Up

If you're talking to a customer and he has his eye on someone else, try agreeing, "Oh yeah, she is really beautiful." Then throw in a good quality about yourself. "With her tits and my ass, we make the perfect woman. Why not get the best of both worlds tonight?"

Tag-teaming men can work wonders. Its hard enough to resist one beautiful woman - two is damn near impossible. Play Good Cop, Bad Cop; Shy & Wild; Ebony & Ivory; Secret Lesbian Lovers. Any duo schtick you can dream up and pull off - use it.

Make sure your scam partner is aware of your personal boundaries, strategies, and expected tip amounts, in order to finesse the best for both of you. You can also sell a 'double dance' to customers with the two of you at one time. Set the price together.

When Making it Rain Evaporates

If you dance on the floor with a group of other dancers, discuss upfront how you will split the cash. Grab your own as it falls? Put it all in a bucket and figure it out afterwards? How many dancers are in the cut? This situation can quickly turn into a clusterfuck that ends up divided too many ways, and dancers make very little money. You can always opt out.

Knuck if You Buck

Strippers can be protective of their customers, and aggressive towards other dancers. You are free to talk to and dance for whoever you want. But be prepared to assert yourself to other dancers and back up your autonomy. Strip club dressing rooms are places where its not unusual for dancers to be beaten with padlocks. Know who you're dealing with, where you fall in the food chain, and how hard you really are.

IT CAN HAPPEN TO YOU:

New or naive waitresses can ruin your up-sell potential if they don't understand the psychology of sales.

Audrey was doing an hour suite with Omar, a customer who was very susceptible to her sales suggestions. As the time neared the end, she began to use the tactics in this book to secure an additional hour. She had almost closed the sale when a new waitress, Patricia, burst in the rom.

Patricia flicked on the lights and screeched, "Times up!" The customer snapped back to reality. Audrey tried to perform damage control, and flicked the lights back off.

"Hey Patty, Omar and I are interested in spending another hour together," Audrey said, while sitting down on the customer's lap and motioning the waitress toward her.

Patricia stupidly said, "Ok, I'll wait outside so you don't feel pressured while you decide, Omar."

Patricia killed the mood *and* the save for a second sale. That meant Audrey lost money, and Patricia ruined an opportunity to secure an additional tip for herself.

Teach your waitress partners a few things about closing additional room sales before running suites. Explain how a better option is joining the room with a sexy cleavage strip tease and purring, "Looks like we're going to need to keep the fun going for another hour, sexy." Button up as the transaction is approved.

RATCHET TIP:

Anyone who works at the club has the potential to put you on and connect you with a big spender. Feel free to tip them at your discretion if they literally put $1k-$2k directly in your hands. Otherwise, keep your money to yourself and *don't depend on other people for your hustle.*

BEWARE:

Law are laws, but at the end of the day, this is the seedy strip club underworld. If you cause too many problems, the club will simply fire you, or send your tax info to the IRS. Stand up for yourself - but know how far you can press each issue at your club before they retaliate. Be strategic. Pick your battles.

8 STAYING SOBER

Customers want dancers to get fucked up. This means lower inhibitions, and allowing more than you would if you were sober. They want you fucked up so they can take advantage of you, sexually assault you, and rape you - point blank. Don't get it twisted, and don't let your guard down.

Whatever you do for fun in your personal life, keep it in your personal life. Stay safe, healthy, sober, and in good working condition at the club. When you are sober, you are in control. When you are in control, you get paid. That's the whole reason you go to the club: to get paid; not to party.

Be An Award-Winning Actress

Do not get fucked up at the club. *Pretend*, but don't do it. You are an actress, first and foremost.

Play into the act of ordering drinks, saying things like, "Tequila makes my clothes fall off!" Or when selling suites where a free bottle of bubbly is included, tell them, "Champagne makes me naughty!" Get excited about shots. Even request them. Remember, your persona is dumb, happy, wanna have fun, and wanna get fucked up. Its what they want, so give it to them - or so they think.

Alcohol Can Be Your (Fake) Friend

Pretend to take your shots, pretend to drink your drinks, and pretend to be drunk. The customer will be happy, and you will be sober.

Throw the shots over your shoulder while the customer isn't looking. Spit them back into a chaser cup. Order fake virgin drinks. Pretend to do lines of cocaine, but blow it away. Do anything you have to do in order to pretend you're getting fucked up. But don't actually get fucked up!

Don't Trade a $1000 Night for a Hangover and a Wet Ass

If you get fucked up, you get fucked. Literally and figuratively. Dancers get drunk, snort a few lines, give things away for free, and waste the whole night. They recover the next day, regret it for life, and usually have no money to show for it.

Be disciplined. You are at work. You are your own boss. You can make infinite money. Do not waste these opportunities. Stay sober, alert, and get that cash.

Tricks to Avoid Drinking Alcohol

If you can get away with it, wear a wristband and say you're underage.

With drinks, you can pretend to do a shot with the customer. Order a coke back first, and take a couple of sips to lower the amount of liquid in the glass. Make sure your hand is cupping the glass so the customer can't see how full it is.

Take the shot, but hold the liquor in your mouth and spit it back into the chaser glass without swallowing. The best position for this is sitting on the customer's lap facing away from them, so they can't see you very well. If you can't get your hands on a chaser in time, try the Coyote Ugly[34] trick: steal the guy's beer and spit your shot in it while pretending to use it as a chaser.

Order fake drinks. At one club, any drinks ordered with the name 'Passion' included were known by staff to be non-alcoholic. But to the customer, it sounds like you're getting fucked up.

COCAINE

Identified by:

"Do you like to party?"
Party favors
White

---

[34] American romantic musical comedy-drama film based on the Coyote Ugly Saloon.

Powder
Sugar
Coke
Powder your nose

Cokeheads are Basically the Ideal Customer

Customers love to come to the strip club to do cocaine. They want you to do it, too. *Don't.* Stay sober in the club. But you can pretend, and make a shit ton of money off of them in the process. Cocaine will keep him horny and excited to be with you for hours on end in private suites, but prevent his dick from getting hard so he can't rape you. Milk this situation for all its worth.

Cokeheads can be annoying, but are usually bottomless money pits. They know their habit requires large stacks of cash, and they normally spend freely when fucked up. They will want to do line after line. You can distract them temporarily by having them do lines off of your ass or tits, but eventually they will want you to join in the fun.

If you say "No thanks, I don't do that," your participation in the party (and money) will be abruptly cut off. Many dancers will join him simply to be paid in snorting cocaine all night. *Don't be that girl.* Play him and get your money.

Advanced Savagery

When its time for 'your line,' bend over in front of him to do it. Dance for him with your ass in his face. He will be distracted by you.

Take the rolled bill (tell him its bad luck to use anything less than a $20 - and especially good luck for a $100), bring it to your mouth and nose area, and simply breathe out heavily instead of sniffing inwards. The cocaine disappears into thin air, and the noise sounds as if you did the line. Pocket the rolled bill. He will produce a new one every time.

If there is no bill, do some fake nail bumps. Stick two fingers into the powder, and blow on one. Voila.

Stay away from the dancers who actually do drugs at the club. Drama follows them. If you hang around them, men who are used to paying in drugs and fucking for free will now look to you for those services, because birds of a feather flock together.

IT CAN HAPPEN TO YOU:

A Tale of Two Strippers

A customer asked Ciara and Koko to do an hour suite with them. The customer 'liked to party.' Ciara pretended to get fucked up, using the techniques outlined in this book, but Koko really drank her drinks, took her shots, and sniffed her lines. Ciara kept her head in the game, working the room, entertaining the customer, pouring champagne, dancing, and keeping her safe distance.

Koko ended up trashed very quickly. In her fucked up stupor, she forgot she was at work. Instead of maintaining her boundaries, she allowed the customer to kiss and finger her. She then ended up running out of the suite to vomit backstage in the dressing room, and passed out for the rest of her shift.

Still sober, Ciara finished the suite with the customer. Since Koko had let him do whatever he wanted, the customer tried to push Ciara past her boundaries. She smiled and flirted, but softly told him in no uncertain terms she "wasn't that kind of girl, and hoped he enjoyed the time he spent with her anyway." Of course he said he did, and she hustled a nice tip out of him. Then Ciara went back on the floor to make more money.

RATCHET TIP: Perfect your 'tipsy routine.' You can get away with being spoiled, and asking for a lot of money and gifts, while 'under the fake influence.' Acting skills are key.

BEWARE: Cocaine, and other narcotics, are illegal, but they are also rampant in strip clubs. Do what you will, but beware. Waitresses have been busted for selling coke to undercover cops in suites. Also, partying 'just at work' can turn into an expensive addiction that not only ruins your life, but leaves you broke.

9 SANITARY STUFF

Although it may close for a few hours for a cleaning crew to do a once-over, the strip club is a dirty place. The gross reality is that the couches, carpet, and chairs have been coated in everything from vomit and semen, to saliva and piss. Limit your exposure.

Dirty Club = Butt Pimples

You never want to sit your bare butt or skin on the dirty club chairs, if you can help it. Bring a blanket or towel for your dressing room chair. When on the floor, don't sit directly on the chairs and bar stools. Wear a sexy lingerie robe, or kneel. Always wear shoes in the dressing room. Wipe down your makeup counter area backstage (the club should provide cleaner).

Shower thoroughly after work every night, and wash every part of your body. Far too many dancers want to save last night's face beat, or are 'too tired to shower,' before hitting the hay. Its gross, will clog the pores on your body, cause acne, and turn your bed into a swamp of bacteria. Have an after-work routine to ensure you take a damn shower, and get good rest in clean sheets.

Washing Work Panties is Non-Negotiable

Wash your work clothes often. This is not like other work uniforms where you can go a few days in-between. WASH YOUR WORK PANTIES AFTER EVERY SINGLE SHIFT. The easiest way is to hand wash them in the sink, and hang them to air dry.

You Can Get Herpes Through Lip Gloss

Use your own makeup. Never borrow another dancer's makeup. Watch out for the makeup artists as well - they often reuse the same applicators on multiple dancers. This is never a good idea. DO NOT SHARE makeup, lip gloss, cigarettes, pipes, kisses, drinks, or anything you put your mouth on!

Disease, infections, and herpes are real and communicable. Once your health is compromised, there's no turning back. Take care of yourself and make good decisions. Wipe your body down frequently with baby wipes or hand sanitizer.

IT CAN HAPPEN TO YOU:

Stassia was excited to be invited to join a big spender suite by bossy Mercedes, a veteran dancer at the club. Mercedes gave some words of advice, let her borrow a more high class outfit, and "fixed her makeup for her," adding a nude Victoria Secret gloss to Stassia's already plump lips. Stassia woke up a few days later to blisters on her lips, from unknowingly sharing Mercedes' lip gloss during an outbreak. Now Stasssia has oral herpes for life.

RATCHET TIP: To dry work panties in a hurry: 1. Turn the heat on high, full blast, and place the g-string on a car vent on the way to work; 2. Wrap the g-string around a hair blowdryer at a high setting and let sit to dry; 3. Place the g-string in a paper towel and sit on top of the cosmetic bulb mirror lighting in dressing room.

BEWARE: The strip club is not a place you want to be with an open wound. You could get a staph infection, among other things. Stay home if you need to, and use bandages and wrap if you *must* come to work.

10 MONEY

TELL NO ONE ABOUT YOUR MONEY

The more you work, the more you will fall into the 'stripper world,' where nothing seems expensive or out of reach. You have the option to go to the club at any time, hustle as hard and long as you can, and come home with stacks to take care of whatever you need. This will never be the case for the majority of your non-stripper friends.

Most people associate anxiety, stress, and despair with money. They are unlikely to experience the financial security you feel. And they will *not* be happier knowing you have a surplus of thousands of dollars, can buy whatever you want, and do whatever you choose with your time. Some might become envious. A select few may even decide to rob you.

You might not believe that could happen to you, but people do unexpected things out of desperation. Be safe carrying your cash! Don't tell anyone you have cash on you or in your house! *Nobody needs to know how much money you make.*

WHAT TO DO WITH YOUR MONEY

Secure The Bag

Always secure your money right away when you're on the floor. Put money either in your bag, garter, sock, or wrapped around your rubber bands. When your stash gets too big, discretely drop it off in your locker backstage, and make sure to lock it.

Keep Cashing Out

Cash out any dance dollars immediately. The club may tell you they are good for a certain period of time, but ignore that and cash them out as soon as possible. If you're in a suite, take a bathroom break to secretly cash them out at the cage.[35]

There are no guarantees. A customer may attempt to cancel a suite halfway through. You could get fired. The club may close overnight. *Always cash out your certificates right away*, even if you have to take home thousands of ones. You should be able to exchange them for big bills within days.

Create a Paper Trail

If you want to be approved for things such as mortgages, lines of credit, and auto loans, you must create a history of work income. To do this, you need to deposit money into a bank account on a regular basis. A good habit is going directly to the bank or ATM after each shift.

Keep track of your income and expenses on a calendar. This can help you remember what you made and when, as well as identify patterns for high earning times throughout the year.

Tax Time

Keep receipts for all work expenses, including hair appointments, costumes, makeup, gym memberships, and anything related to your appearance or work duties. Many of these items are tax deductible and can lower your taxable income significantly.

Hire an experienced tax accountant. Make sure they take advantage of entertainer's deductible expenses. Look into paying quarterly taxes so you don't end up owing thousands at the end of the year.

Be Smart With Your Money

Save money for slow seasons (right after Christmas, tax time, first hint of patio weather), days when you don't want to go to work, unexpected illnesses, and emergencies.

Invest your money in something for the future. Do you have a business idea? Want to become a real estate tycoon? Open your own nail salon?

---

[35] Locked area where club staff handles cash, including receiving house fees, and cashing out dance dollars.

Fund your full-time art career? The strip club is the perfect place to raise your own capital. You don't need a fancy third-party investor to green light your passion project - bankroll it yourself!

What NOT to Do With Your Money

Do not put your money on social media unless you want to get robbed. Straight up. It happens all the time.

Don't tell anyone at work, home, or *anywhere,* how much money you make. Jealousy is strange. Even if someone isn't stealing cash from you outright, they could be overcharging you, or ask to borrow money with no intent of ever paying it back, "because you have so much money."

Don't tip out all of your money (see **Becoming a Stripper, Ch. 1**). Take care of yourself first.

Don't buy expensive work clothes. Men want to rip $15 Walmart lingerie off of you just as much as $150 Victoria's Secret teddies. Oftentimes, other strippers are getting rid of (new or used) clothing and shoes backstage, and are more than happy to either give it to you for free, or sell it at a deep discount (see **What to Wear, Ch. 2**).

Don't buy expensive work makeup. Men don't know the difference between Chanel and Cover Girl. Also, don't reapply late at night. Customers are fucked up, and they don't care.

Some dancers don't even wear makeup and make bank. Princess loved doing a full face beat for work, and spent over $2,200 on Kylie Lip Kits in 2016. But she made even more money the next year after she ditched the makeup, deciding she was beautiful enough to dance barefaced.

Mi Hungrii

Don't buy anything at work with your own money. Avoid the vending machine! Bring snacks or have customers buy you food. Don't let customers feed you bar food - demand they bring healthy meals and vegan fare. Take advantage of them. Don't go out to eat after work every night, or get fast food on the way home. Bring your own jug of water to work.

C.R.E.A.M.

If you're cash based, set up an envelope system. Portion out your earnings for different bills after each shift - about 90 percent of what you make - and only spend the left over one dollar bills (or another minimal amount).

Pay bills in cash or mail money orders. Use prepaid cash cards for necessary online and in-person payments.

How to Fly Under the Radar

Obtain a safe deposit box where you can privately and securely store your cash - without questions from the government.

Do not deposit your money into your bank account in large lump sums (or multiple, frequent deposits totaling $10k), unless you want the IRS to be notified.

Do not make large purchases over $9,999 unless you want the IRS to be notified. If you want to buy a car, you can pay a cash down payment that reduces the loan amount to $9,999 or less, to avoid your finances being flagged.

IT CAN HAPPEN TO YOU:

Salina loved Nate, her boyfriend of two years. But it was clear to anyone looking from the outside-in that he was holding her back. Nate could barely keep a part-time job, and was always asking Salina for money. His car needed new brakes, he was late on his rent, and always wanted to go out to eat.

"What's the big deal? You make hundreds of dollars a night," he would say, as he finessed Salina out of her hard-earned money. The more she agreed to help, the more helpless he became, and the more he asked for money.

She ended up broke each week, having to work extra shifts just to pay her regular bills. Salina had to cut off her leeching boyfriend, who had decided to lean on her, instead of being responsible, putting in the work, and taking care of himself.

As soon as she spent her time, energy, and money on herself, Salina realized how much money she actually made, and was able to focus it toward her own goals. Her bills were always paid on time, her car loan paid off, and she experienced financial freedom.

Let everyone be responsible for themselves. If they want to make the money you make, they can go out and do the work that you do. Keep your money.

RATCHET TIP: Envelopes in mattresses (or the updated version, cash in a locked, fireproof safe box) work just as well in the 2000s as they did back in the day. *Tell no one!*

BEWARE: The government, customers, club, and all the staff will attempt to separate you from your money. Be smart with your money. You worked for it. Make sure you keep it.

The club may send a 1099 form to you and the IRS. Find out if they do! If so, you must declare at the minimum, the income listed on the 1099, and offset it with deductible expenses on your taxes.

11 GROUPS AND COUPLES

Groups

The key to groups is to attack them as a whole, and get them to nominate each other for dances - because men always buckle under peer pressure! Do a dance for one, and he will sell you to the rest.

Get the attention of the group, introduce yourself, and ask them who needs a lap dance the most. They will do your job for you and point out the weakest link in the group. Take him for a dance.

If nobody volunteers, say, "So since I don't have a volunteer, does that mean *I get to choose*?" in an excited voice. Ponder a bit, and pay close attention to who keeps eye contact with you. Then say, "Well, if I get to choose, then I choose *you*!" Flash a big smile, and grab his hand. "Let's go."

Or, "So guys, if I took Sebastien for a dance, would you miss him too much? No? Well, okay then. Let's go Sebastien!" You can also say, "Ok guys, I'm kidnapping Hans and making him my sex slave and never bringing him back!" They will encourage him to go with you.

Once I get the first guy in a group to go for a dance, I bring him back and say, "Shea was a perfect gentleman. Can you believe that, guys? I guess there is a first for everything. Ok, Shea, who would you recommend I dance for next? Should I dance for Andre or Paul? Andre... why? Well that's good enough reason for me. Let's go, Andre!"

Once you're finished with Andre, repeat throughout the entire group. When a guy suggests his friend get a dance, 99 percent of the time, the friend will go. Once you've cycled through the whole group, come back to the well later to see who wants to dance again.

Bachelor Parties

If it's a bachelor party, you'll be told right away. Bachelor parties aren't known to spend a lot, since most of the groomsmen tend to be fairly broke. Your best bet with a bachelor party is to ask who is buying the bachelor the first dance! Have him sell you to the rest of the group after your dance.

Couples

Although they can seem intimidating, couples are in the club to get dances. Its always good to look for people with open body language, who clearly want you to interact with them. However, couples are often nervous. Approach them first. You may be the only dancer who does, and this helps your sales significantly.

Compliment both of them by saying to the man, "You brought your own beautiful girl!" This opens up the conversation from a positive point of view, and allows you to gauge their demeanor. Always ask the lady if you can sit down. "You wouldn't mind if I joined, would you?" while smiling and nodding.

When you sit down, keep the man engaged by making eye contact and saying, "Look at this lucky man, who has a hot lady come to the club with him!"

Focus your attention back on the girl, say, "Whats your name? I love your [top/perfume/hair/boobs/whatever] - you are so sexy!"

They will feel comfortable with you, which not a lot of dancers know how to do with couples. In a club full of dancers who don't approach them in a friendly manner - or at all - you will most likely make a sale. When you hear, "You're our favorite," you know they're sold. If the woman wants you, the guy will open his wallet. It's all about getting the woman to like you.

IT CAN HAPPEN TO YOU:

Bachelor parties can offer an extra way to make money. Leeanna buddied up with the best man and steered him toward the DJ booth to prepay for a Bachelor Dance on stage. She chose a few dancers to perform with her for an extra fee. The club usually pays anywhere from $20 - $50 for bachelor dances.

Onstage bachelor dances alternate between stripping for the bachelor, and beating the shit out of him. Leeanna had his friends pay her ahead of time to give the bachelor a boxer-busting wedgie, and they loved it so much they tipped her an additional $100 afterwards. Make sure you offer them the opportunity to tip you to destroy their friend!

RATCHET TIP: Never discount. Make sure to charge double for a dance as a couple. If a dance is regularly $50, its at least $100 for a couple.

BEWARE: Women can be worse than the men with roving hands and mouths. They justify this by saying, "We're girls, its fine!" *Hell no.* Sexual assault is sexual assault - from a woman or a man. Women need to respect your boundaries, too! Keep an extra eye on them.

12 REGULARS

Regulars[36] can provide a steady stream of income, gifts, food deliveries, and a lifeline to save you from owing house rent when the club is dead. They can also be the source of stress, unreasonable demands, and invasion of privacy. Regulars are a double-edged sword, and reaping the benefits of a regular requires a significant investment of time and emotional labor.

Trap Phone

Its helpful to have some sort of contact to give out to potential regulars, so you can call them in on bad nights. Pre-paid phones are especially good for this. All of your personal info is secure, but your customers can still be in touch.

Leave your schedule each week on the voicemail of your trap phone, or send it out in a text to your regulars, with lots of kissy emojis. That way they'll know when you'll be at the club, and you don't have to spend time talking to them personally on your off days.

Its All in the Details

Always, always, always make sure you remember little details about your regulars. It makes them feel special, which is the key to maintaining the faux relationship. When you are spending time with them, they should feel like the most important person in the room, if not the world.

Follow up on the work trip they took to San Francisco since you last saw

---

[36] Customer who returns to the strip club repeatedly to spend money with you.

them. Ask about their pet, Charlie the Chihuahua, by name. Order their favorite drink, *"neat,"* just how they like it. If you need to save info on your phone or write it in a notebook - do it! Just remember to remember.

Its a Date!

Set a date with the customer. "I can't wait to see you Wednesday. I'll be waiting in my pink panties at 9pm." It puts the idea into their head and makes seeing you a priority. You're making it known that you're not concerned about the other people in the club, and you're going to be there just to see *him*.

NEVER MEET REGULARS OUTSIDE THE CLUB

Don't fuck this up. Number one, its not safe. Number two, we all lose money.

Tricks should not be able to enjoy your company simply by taking you to dinner. If they want the privilege of your time, they need to spend a few racks on you in the club, where you have the set prices, safety, and no-sex policy to keep you protected. Once customers get you outside of the club, they will *always* try to give you less money, while simultaneously demanding more from you.

You're doing yourself a disservice by allowing customers to interact with you outside of the club in the real world. A job is a job and a trick is a trick. Get that cash and keep them where they belong: inside the trap.

IT CAN HAPPEN TO YOU:

Regulars can be nice to have, but not essential. Peaches worked for five years with no regulars, just selling to new customers every shift. She didn't like the emotional labor involved with regulars, or the inability to charge them for each annoying text message. She wasn't interested in having someone pay her monthly light bill. Peaches just wanted the cash, and she was gone. It is 100 percent possible to work without regulars.

RATCHET TIP: If you do have a regular, work toward a large monetary goal. Whether its a '$6k down payment for a car,' '$9k boob job,' or '$20k for tuition,' - plant the seeds, and watch them manifest!

BEWARE: Don't get caught up investing too much into regulars. Texts are time-consuming. Is it really worth it? Remember, everything costs! Find a way to monetize, or cut them loose.

13 MANIFESTING

Learn about and activate intention, the law of attraction, and manifestation. Study Abraham Hicks, Bob Proctor, Think and Grow Rich, and the like. Develop an abundance mindset. Be grateful for the flexible job you have, and the money you make - while always being ready for, and expecting to receive, more.

Bring In Your Own Vibe

There is always money to be made at the strip club; whether its a Monday afternoon, or a Saturday night. Ignore other dancers at work. Use headphones in the dressing room to block out drama. Do not participate in negativity. *There are no bad days.*

It doesn't matter what other dancers made that day, or how 'slow' it has been. You are not them and they are not you. There are always men coming to the strip club to spend money on you. Your customer is on their way.

Pre-Pussy Popping Playlists

Headphones block out the downers in the dressing room. Replace them with positive reinforcement. Try searching YouTube for money, luck, and abundance frequencies. Listen to these while visualizing yourself receiving cash to become a money magnet.

Empowered female artists, who embrace and celebrate their sexuality, can also help get in the money-making mood. Try OG Gangsta Boo,[37] Mia X, [38] Trina,[39] Cardi B, Madonna,[40] and your personal favorites.

Thinking of a Master Plan

Consider how many hours you have during a shift. Calculate how much money you would make if you consistently sold dances in-between stage sets. For an 8-hour shift, if you sold one set of three for $100 dances in-between each set, that's a minimum of $800 from dances alone. This is an attainable goal minimum per shift. Always be closing.

Tape a dollar inside your locker, and with a sticky note with a financial goal written on it. When the club is slow, or spirits are down, remind yourself of the goal by looking at or meditating on the sticky note and dollar. Then return to the floor, refreshed and focused.

Stripping Training Tools

There are a plethora of stripping resources available, including: Stripper Web Forum,[41] Racks to Riches,[42] and Survive the Club,[43] to name a few. Take advantage of the free resources, and use some of your cash to order their books and training tools. Support the dancers spreading sales advice to help you earn more.

IT CAN HAPPEN TO YOU:

Piper made friends with dancers who loved to complain. They sat together backstage, did each other's makeup, and hyped up all the drama. They talked so much about how "the club is dead 'till 3am," that Piper just chilled with

---

[37] American rapper from Memphis, Tennessee. First and only female member of Three 6 Mafia. "The Devil's Daughter." Playlist: "Where Dem Dollas At?" and "Can I Get Paid?"

[38] American rapper from New Orleans, songwriter and actress. First female emcee to have a contract on Master P's No Limit Records. "Mother of Southern Gangsta Rap." Playlist: "The Party Don't Stop"

[39] American rapper and television personality from Florida. "Da Baddest Bitch." Playlist: "Pull Over" and "Da Baddest Bitch."

[40] American singer, songwriter actress, and businesswoman. "Queen of Pop." Playlist: "Human Nature" and "Hung Up."

[41] Exotic Dancer Community where strippers can learn from each other and share information. www.stripperweb.net

[42] Sales training for strippers: all about growing your dancing business, with training, tools, worksheets, and exercises to help you grow. www.rackstoriches.com

[43] Website sharing information on how to become a stripper. www.survivetheclub.com

them in the dressing room for hours, complaining how slow it was.

Meanwhile, Sugar hustled on the floor from 8p - 12a. She picked up $675 in that same time period Piper wasted. Your mindset determines your actions, which determine your outcome

RATCHET TIP:

Write down your money goal with a pen and paper and say it outloud: "I am going to make $$$$ tonight. In exchange I will offer smiles, conversation, jokes, and lap dances. I will make people feel important. Men will approach me with respect, follow my rules, and tip me lavishly."

Meditate on your ideal shift and monetary outcome before you go to work. Visualize what you wrote out - meeting receptive customers who are tipping you lots of cash. Feel the excitement and rush of adrenaline as you count your money at the end of your shift. Go to work ready to receive your monetary goal.

BEWARE: Make sure your shift goal is high enough, but don't fixate on a certain number too much. The money will come. However, do not fall into the "it all evens out, sometimes you make $1000, sometimes you make $0," trap. *NO!*

You don't work as a stripper for it to "even out." You work as a stripper to earn bank. Keep your faith in yourself strong, goals high, and work ethic in check. Be grateful for the opportunity to make your own salary.

14 MONEY IGN

You can tell when a customer likes you. Pay attention to their body language. Watch their posture, facial expressions, and hand movements. Are they leaning towards you? Did you catch them checking out your body? Are their pupils dilated? Is their hand resting on your leg or back?

When customers say the following, you know for sure money is coming your way:

"Wow, you're just what I've been looking for all night!"

"How much is VIP?"

"I won/lost $$$$ last night gambling." It doesn't matter if they won or lost, because if they could afford to lose several thousand dollars and still go out the next night, they have money to burn.

"I'm staying at the Ritz-Carlton [or some other high-end hotel]."

When they are facilitating an experience for a group, such as a work trip, "What's your name? Great, Brooklyn? I'm Warren. Do you have a friend for Ian here?"

Me: "How are you?"
Him: "Better now!"
= $$$$$$$$

"So, how does this work?" "What's the deal here?" and "Ok, so what are my options?" are *always* followed by lots of money.

"I just got into town on business."

IT CAN HAPPEN TO YOU:

Lula approached a shy looking customer sitting alone at the bar. He was receptive to her introduction and offered to buy her a drink shortly after she sat down. She couldn't tell whether or not he was going to spend, until one of his first questions was, "Can you tell me how this works?"

Lula heard the Money $ign and smiled. She said, "Sure," and explained the club from the top (suites and dances, including usual amounts of gratuity for dancers) to bottom (tipping on stage). He thanked her, and confessed it was his first time at a strip club. He was creating his own private bachelor party do-over, since his was "so boring and family-friendly" the previous weekend.

He asked Lula to do an hour suite with him, and she said, "I'd love to." Since she already explained the club to him through her preferred lens, he was respectful, didn't press her boundaries, tipped her a minimum of $100 per half hour before the suite, and an additional tip after. They both had a good time.

RATCHET TIP: Once you identify a Money $ign, act immediately! Time is money - don't waste it. If the customer indicates they are ready and willing to spend - take them for all they've got - *now!* There is no reason to wait and waste time.

BEWARE: Some men know how to drag *you* along - feigning interest in suites, hinting about having or dropping lots of cash, but never making it rain or swiping the card. Don't let them fool you. Know when to cut your losses and move on to the next customer.

15 AVOIDING BURNOUT

Burn Out

Being a stripper is a stressful job, and burn out is real. When your body is exhausted, or you have an attitude with every customer, its time to take a break. One of the best perks of the job is the schedule flexibility. Take some time off and go unwind at a beach. You'll feel brand new when you get back.

Sleep

Make sure you get enough sleep. Quality and quantity are both important. It needs to be consecutive and uninterrupted, for 6-8 hours. Your body is working hard, and awake strange hours when you really should be asleep, because your organs need to replenish and heal during those times.

If you work night shift, your body may want to be awake during the daytime, but discipline yourself to get enough rest. You may require blackout curtains. Get creative and cover your windows in foil, or whatever you have to do to block out the light. Your body needs to be tricked into thinking it is nighttime and dark out. Make sure you go to sleep at night on your off days.

Use a white noise or rain app to block out noises, help you relax, and stay asleep. A silk weighted eye cover is helpful to keep light out. Guided wind down meditations post after-work shower can help transition you from grind time to rest time.

Pamper Your Body & Mind

Get full-body massages frequently. Make sure you add the cost of a massage into your work goal the night before. Sensory Deprivation Floats can also help your muscles and joints relax and repair.

See a therapist. Sex workers go through a lot. They need someone to talk to. Journaling can help by writing it all out. Sex workers must deal with the trauma they experience daily, in order to stay mentally and emotionally healthy.

Stay Grounded

Don't let the club change you, and don't let it consume your life. Spend time with people who have nothing to do with the strip club. Remind yourself there are men who do not go to strip clubs frequently.

Do fun things. Don't let life turn into sleeping and working. Always remember *why* you work at the club - to enjoy your life, have more time with family, fund passion projects, and travel. Keep doing it! The club will be there when you get back.

IT CAN HAPPEN TO YOU:

Scarlett worked at the Golden Pussy for almost three years. She was at the end of her rope, arguing with staff, beefing with the dancers, and giving customers attitude 24/7. She swore she was leaving and never coming back, but ended her contract with the club on good terms.

She went to work at different clubs in other states, where the rent was too damn high, dances were too damn low, tip outs were crazy, and dancers were doing too much. Scarlett returned to her home club 1.5 years later, with renewed appreciation. Since she was still in the director's good graces, she was welcomed back with open arms.

RATCHET TIP: Have a customer fund you a solo trip out of town to recharge, promising to be extra grateful when you return

BEWARE: Don't burn bridges for no reason! No matter how you feel, you may change your mind later and want to come back to a club. Keep your options open.

ABOUT THE AUTHOR

Blake de Louis is a stripper making six-figures from the Midwest to Manhattan. She has been a high-earner in clubs including: Penthouse, Diamond Cabaret, Scores, Hoops Cabaret, Hollywood, and more.

Contact BlakeDeLouis@gmail.com to book one-on-one dancer training, as well as club-wide trainings for dancers and staff.

www.ingramcontent.com/pod-product-compliance
Lightning Source LLC
Chambersburg PA
CBHW032359280326
41935CB00008B/635